HOLIDAY LINE-UPS

By MizFitz

Leisure Arts • Maumelle Arkansas

PLASTIC CANVAS BASICS

WORKING WITH PLASTIC CANVAS

Counting Threads. Throughout this leaflet, the lines of the canvas will be referred to as threads. However, they are not actually "threads" since the canvas is not woven. Before cutting out your pieces, note the thread count of each chart. The thread count is listed above the chart and indicates the number of threads in the width and height of the canvas pieces. To cut plastic canvas pieces accurately, count **threads** (not **holes**) as shown in **Fig. 1**.

Fig. 1

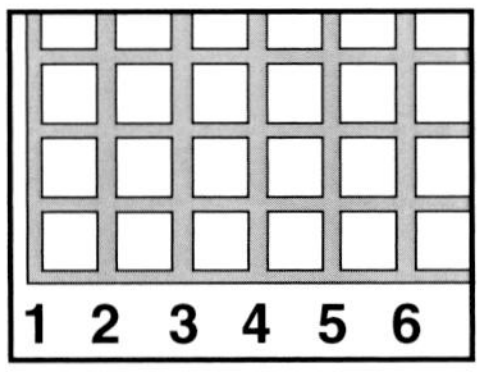

Marking the Canvas. If you find it necessary to mark on the canvas, use an overhead projector pen. Outline shape with pen, cut out shape, and remove markings with water and a towel.

Cutting the Canvas. When cutting canvas, make sure to cut as close to the thread as possible without cutting into the thread. "Nubs" or "pickets" left on the edge of your canvas will snag the yarn and are difficult to cover.

WORKING WITH YARN

Selecting Yarn. We used various brands of worsted weight yarn to stitch the photography models for this leaflet.

Dye Lot Variations. It is important to buy all of the yarn you need to complete your project from the same dye lot; variations between dye lots can be apparent on a stitched piece.

READING THE COLOR KEY

Color keys are included for each project. The heading in each color key is for the descriptive color name (**COLOR**). The key indicates the colors of yarn used and how each color is represented on the chart.

READING THE CHART

Whenever possible, the drawing on the chart looks like the completed stitch. When a stitch cannot clearly be drawn on the chart, like a French knot, a symbol will be used instead. If you have difficulty determining how a particular stitch is worked, refer to Stitch Diagrams.

STITCHING THE DESIGN

Securing the First Stitch. Don't knot the end of your yarn before you begin stitching. Instead, begin each length of yarn by coming up from the wrong side of the canvas and leaving a 1" - 2" tail on the wrong side. Hold this tail against the canvas and work the first few stitches over the tail. When secure, clip the tail close to your stitched piece. Clipping the tail closely is important because long tails can become tangled in future stitches or can show through to the right side of the canvas.

Using Even Tension. Keep your stitching tension consistent, with each stitch lying flat and even on the canvas. Pulling or yanking the yarn causes the tension to be too tight, and you will be able to see through your project. Loose tension is caused by not pulling the yarn firmly enough, and the yarn will not lie flat on the canvas.

Ending Your Stitches. After you've completed all of the stitches of one color in an area, end your stitching by running your needle under several stitches on the back of the stitched piece. To keep the tails of the yarn from showing through or becoming tangled in future stitches, trim the end of the yarn close to the stitched piece.

Stitching Tips

Length of Yarn. It is best to begin stitching with a piece of yarn that is approximately one yard long. However, when working large areas of the same color, you may want to begin with a longer length of yarn to reduce the number of yarn ends and keep the back of your project looking neat.

Keeping Stitches Smooth. Most stitches tend to twist the yarn. Drop your needle and let the yarn untwist every few stitches or whenever needed.

JOINING PIECES

Straight Edges. The most common method of assembling stitched pieces is joining two or more pieces of canvas along a straight edge using overcast stitches. Place one piece on top of the other with right or wrong sides together. Make sure the edges being joined are even, then stitch the pieces together through all layers.

Shaded Areas. The shaded area is part of a chart that has colored shading on top of it. Shaded areas usually mean that all the stitches in that area are used to join pieces of canvas. Do not work the stitches in a shaded area until your project instructions say you should.

Stacking. Sometimes pieces need to be thicker than one layer of canvas. You can do this by stacking. Before you begin stitching, follow your project instructions to stack together plastic canvas pieces so that the edges are even.

Tacking. To tack pieces, run your needle under the backs of some stitches on one stitched piece to secure the yarn. Then run your needle through the canvas or under the stitches on the piece to be tacked in place. The idea is to securely attach your pieces without your tacking stitches showing.

STITCH DIAGRAMS

Unless otherwise indicated, bring threaded needle up at 1 and all odd numbers and down at 2 and all even numbers.

TENT STITCH

This stitch is worked in horizontal or vertical rows over one intersection as shown in **Fig. 2**. Refer to **Fig. 3** to work the reversed tent stitch.

Fig. 2

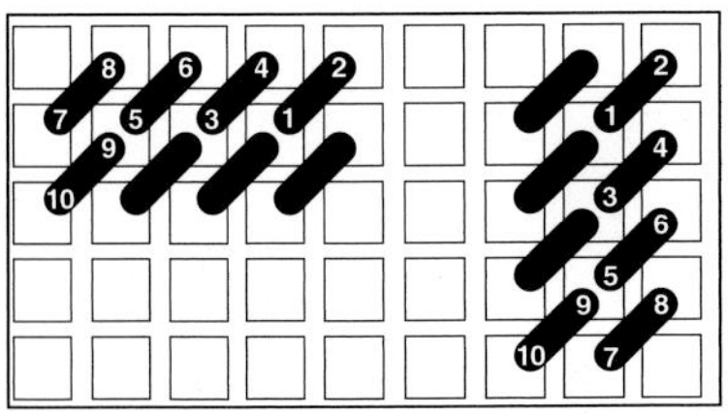

Fig. 3

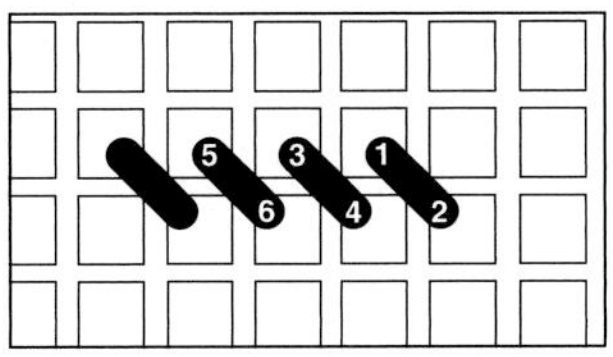

GOBELIN STITCH

This basic straight stitch is worked over two or more threads or intersections (**Fig. 4**). The number of threads or intersections may vary according to the chart.

Fig. 4

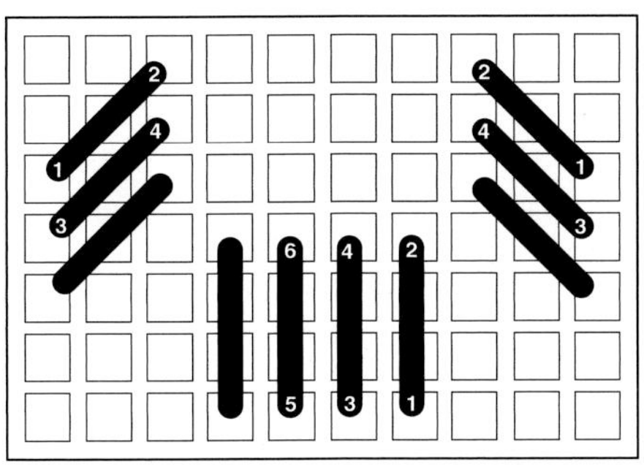

BACKSTITCH

This stitch is worked over completed stitches to outline or define (**Fig. 5**). It is sometimes worked over more than one thread.

Fig. 5

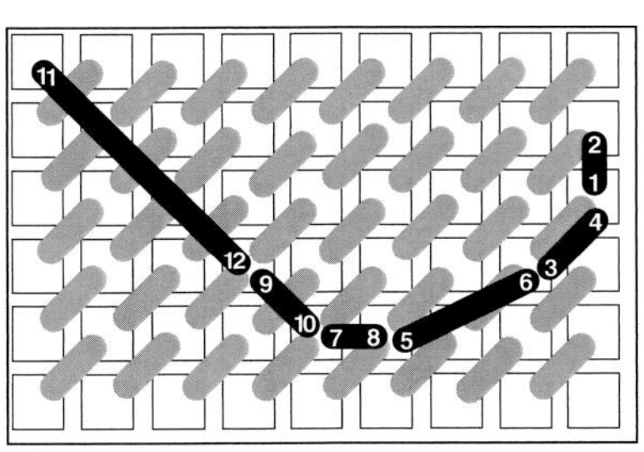

FRENCH KNOT

Come up at 1. Wrap yarn once around needle. Insert the needle at 2 and pull it through the canvas, holding the yarn until it must be released (**Fig. 6**).

Fig. 6

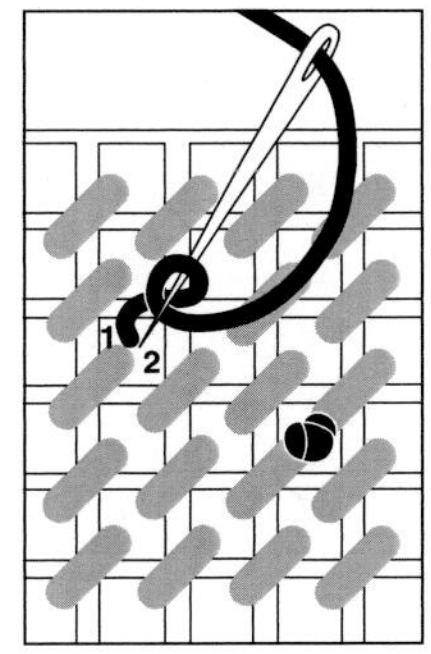

TURKEY LOOP STITCH

This stitch is composed of locked loops. Bring needle up through hole and back down through same hole, forming a loop on top of the canvas. A locking stitch is then made across the thread directly below or to either side of the loop as shown in **Fig. 7**.

Fig. 7

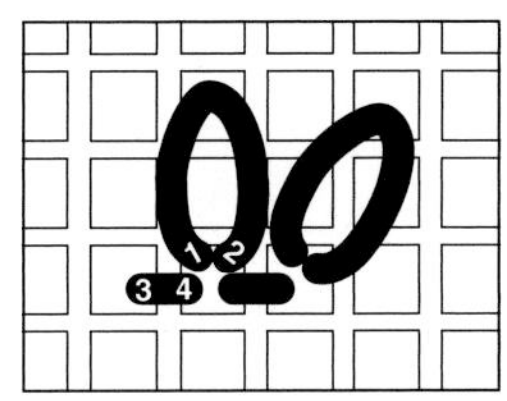

FRINGE STITCH

Fold a 6" length of yarn in half. Thread needle with loose ends of yarn. Bring needle up at 1, leaving a 1" loop on back of the canvas. Go down through loop at 2 (**Fig. 8**). Pull tightly and trim strands 1/2" from knot (**Fig. 9**). A dot of glue on back of fringe will help keep stitches in place.

Fig. 8

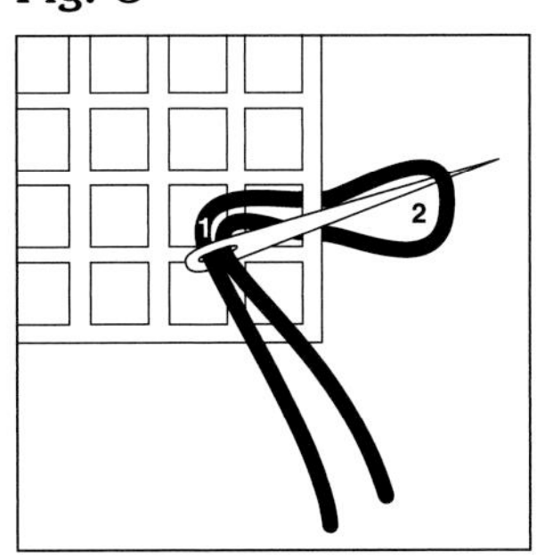

Fig. 9

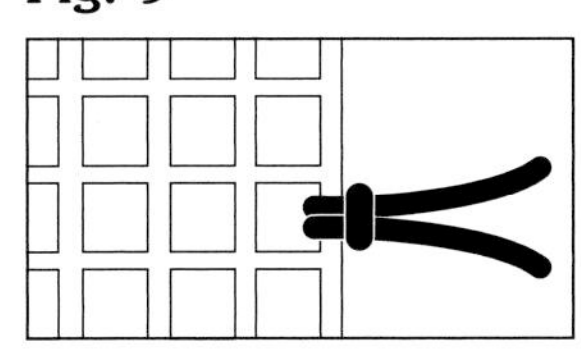

OVERCAST STITCH

This stitch covers the edge of the canvas and joins pieces of canvas (**Fig. 10**). It may be necessary to go through the same hole more than once to get even coverage on the edge, especially at the corners.

Fig. 10

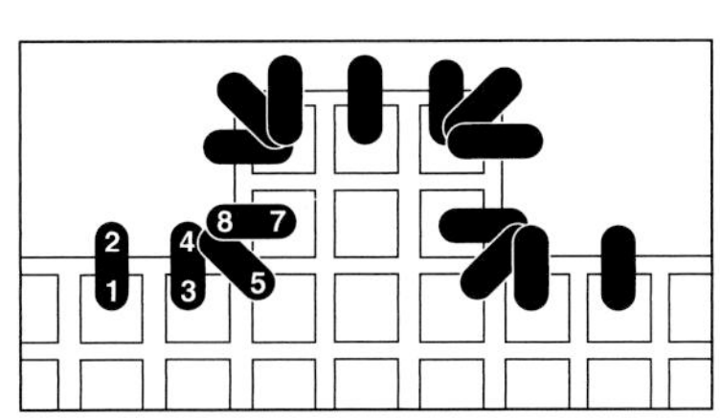

HALLOWEEN

Size: 19$^{1}/_{2}$"w x 13$^{3}/_{4}$"h
Supplies: Worsted weight yarn (refer to color keys), five 10$^{1}/_{2}$" x 13$^{1}/_{2}$" sheets of clear 7 mesh plastic canvas, #16 tapestry needle, four 3" x 10" white foam board rectangles, four 12mm moveable eyes, three 5" lengths of 19 gauge wire, pencil, four dk grey buttons, three purple buttons, powder blush, and craft glue.
Instructions:
You will need to refer to the photo when assembling your Halloween Lineup. Follow charts to cut and stitch Halloween pieces, working backstitches, French knots, and Turkey Loops last and leaving shaded areas unworked.

Frankenstein
1. Tack Eyebrows, Nose, Bolts, and Arms to Frankenstein Front. Glue eyes and grey buttons to Frankenstein Front. Cut a 6" length of black yarn. Loop yarn around Arms; glue ends of yarn to wrong side of Pumpkin. Tack Pumpkin to Frankenstein Front.
2. Matching ★'s, tack top of Shoes to Frankenstein Front. Working stitches in blue shaded area and stitching through three layers of canvas, join Shoes to Frankenstein Front and Back.
3. Placing foam board rectangle between Frankenstein Front and Back, refer to photo for yarn colors and use overcast stitches to join unshaded edges of Frankenstein Front and Back.
4. Tack Ears to edges of Frankenstein Front and Back.

Ghost
1. Tack Bat to Arms; tack Arms to Ghost Front. Tack four diagonal legs of Spider to Ghost Front. Cut a 7$^{3}/_{4}$" length of black yarn; glue yarn to Ghost Front.
2. Matching ♥'s, tack top of Shoes to Ghost Front. Working stitches in blue shaded area and stitching through three layers of canvas, join Shoes to Ghost Front and Back.
3. Placing foam board rectangle between Ghost Front and Back, use white overcast stitches to join unshaded edges of Ghost Front and Back.

Pumpkin Stack
1. Tack two Leaves to the top of each pumpkin.
2. Wrap wire around pencil. Remove the pencil and shape the wire. Glue wire to wrong side of Leaf. Repeat with other two pieces of wire.
3. Placing foam board rectangle between Pumpkin Stack Front and Back, use dk orange overcast stitches to join unshaded edges of Pumpkin Stack Front and Back.

Witch
1. Tack Nose and Arms to Witch Front. Glue eyes and purple buttons to Witch Front.
2. Tack Heart to Bag Front. Matching ■'s, use tan overcast stitches to join Bag Front to Bag Back along unworked edges. Tack Frog to Bag Back. Cut a 6$^{1}/_{2}$" length of tan yarn. Insert yarn through Bag Back from back to front. Loop yarn around Arms and insert yarn through Bag Back from front to back. Secure ends. Glue Bag to Witch Front.
3. Matching ✖'s, work stitches in yellow shaded area to join Hat Brim to Hat. Matching ▲'s and stitching through three layers of canvas, work stitches in green shaded area to join Hat to Witch Front and Back.
4. Matching ♦'s, tack top of Shoes to Witch Front. Place foam board rectangle between Witch Front and Back. Working stitches in blue shaded area and stitching through three layers of canvas, join Shoes to Witch Front and Back. Referring to photo for yarn colors, use overcast stitches to join unshaded edges of Witch Front and Back.
5. Apply blush to Witch's face.

Joining the Lineup
Work stitches in pink shaded areas to cover unworked edges of Fronts only. Insert Hinges in openings on piece sides. Work stitches in grey shaded areas to join Hinges to unworked edges of Backs only.

Hinge
(14 x 7 threads)
(stitch 6)

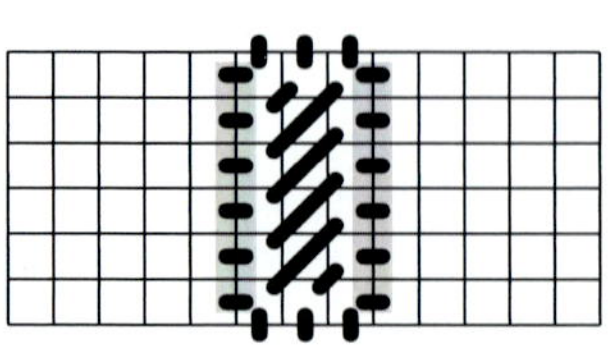

Frankenstein Eyebrow
(4 x 5 threads) (stitch 2)

Pumpkin
(19 x 16 threads)

Frankenstein Nose
(4 x 4 threads) (cut 2)
Stack and stitch through two layers of canvas.

Frankenstein Ear
(3 x 5 threads) (stitch 2)

KEY

COLOR
yellow
orange
dk red
purple
bright green
lt grey
dk grey
black

Frankenstein Front/Back
(30 x 87 threads) (cut 2)
(stitch 1)

Bolt
(8 x 8 threads) (stitch 2)

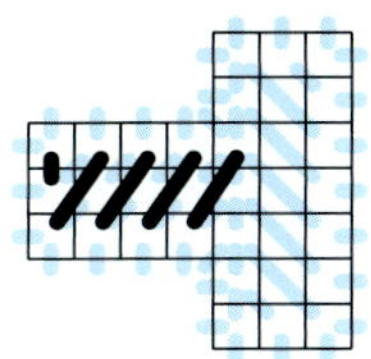

Frankenstein Arms
(30 x 20 threads)

Frankenstein Shoes
(30 x 10 threads)

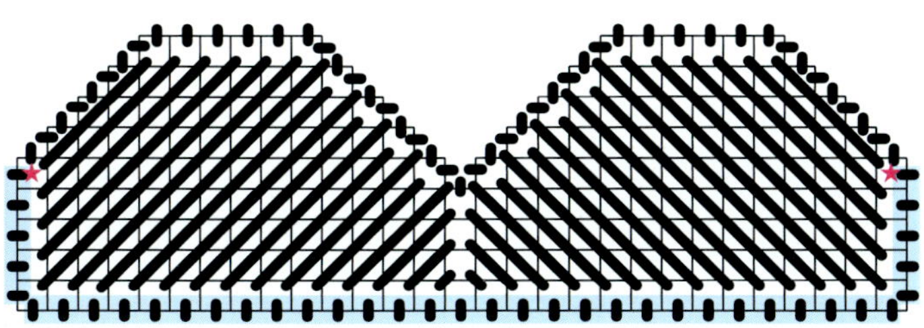

Continued on pg. 6.

Ghost Front/Back
(30 x 84 threads) (cut 2) (stitch 1)

Bat (31 x 12 threads)

Ghost Arms
(30 x 20 threads)

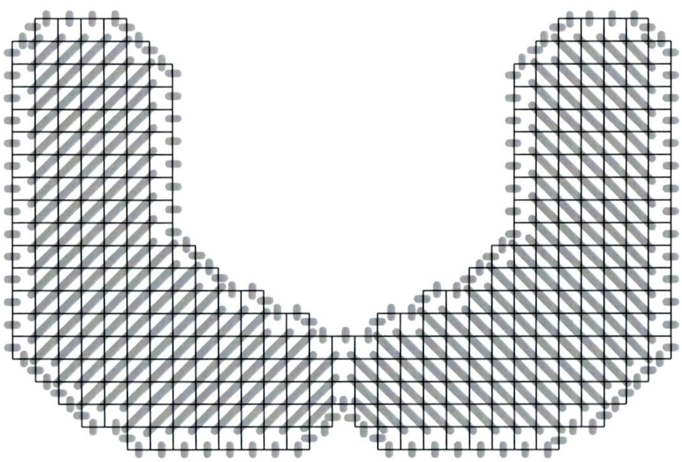

Ghost Shoes
(30 x 10 threads)

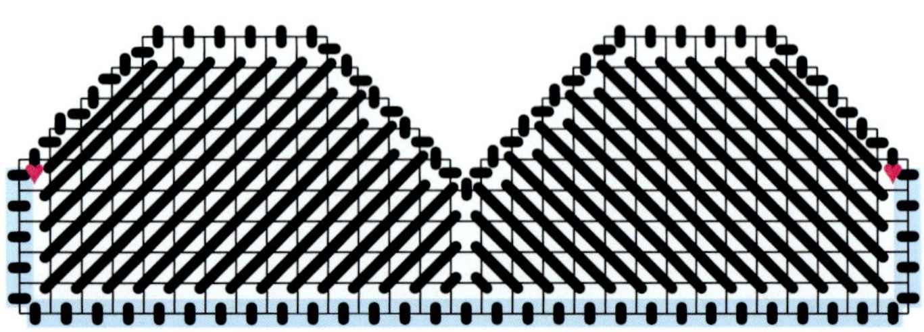

Pumpkin Stack Front/Back
(30 x 87 threads) (cut 2) (stitch 1)

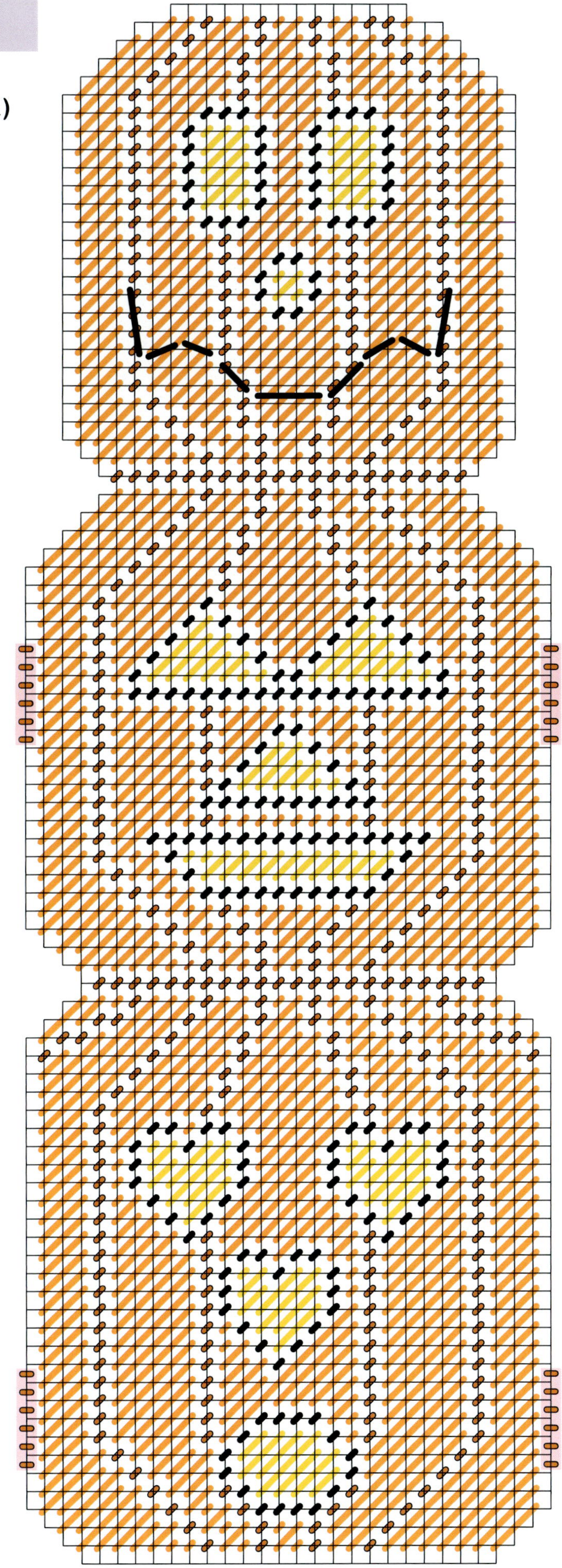

KEY

COLOR
- white
- yellow
- orange
- dk orange
- green
- black
- yellow Fr. knot

Pumpkin Stack Leaf
(6 x 8 threads) (stitch 6)

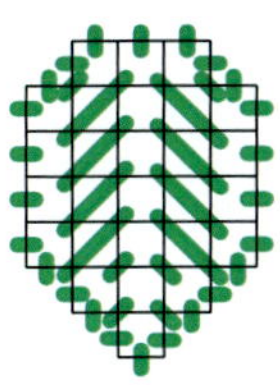

Spider
(12 x 12 threads)

Continued on pg. 8.

HALLOWEEN cont.

KEY

COLOR	COLOR
white	dk green
orange	tan
lt flesh	brown
rose	black
purple	black Fr. knot
bright green	tan Turkey loop

Heart
(10 x 9 threads)

Witch Hat (26 x 22 threads)

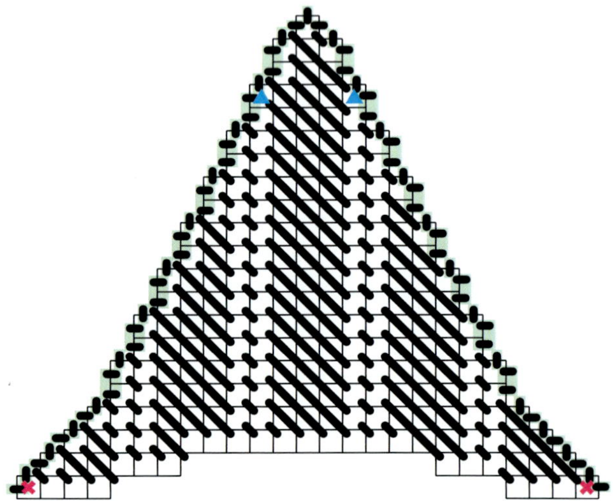

Witch Nose
(4 x 4 threads) (cut 2)
Stack and stitch through two layers of canvas.

Bag Front
(14 x 16 threads)

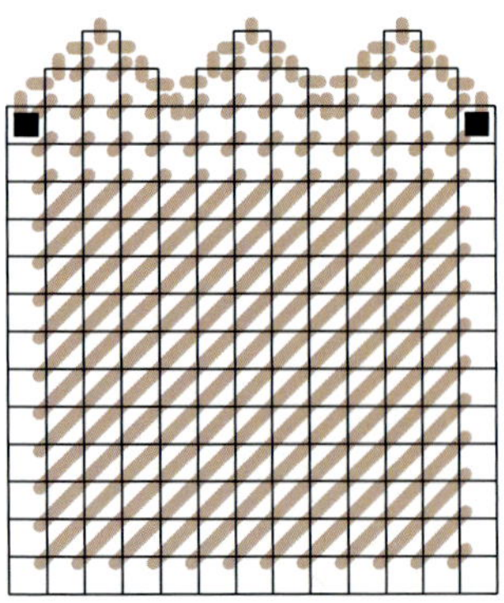

Bag Back
(14 x 18 threads)

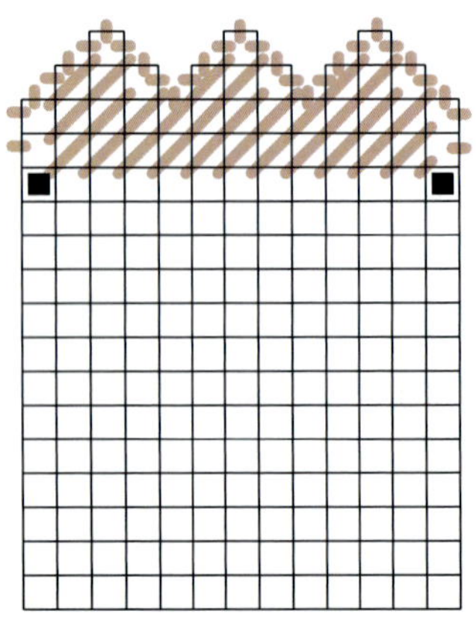

Witch Hat Brim
(34 x 10 threads)

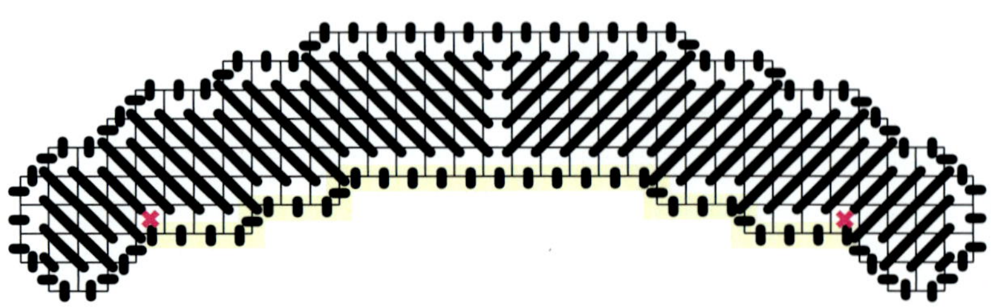

Witch Front/Back
(30 x 90 threads) (cut 2) (stitch 1)

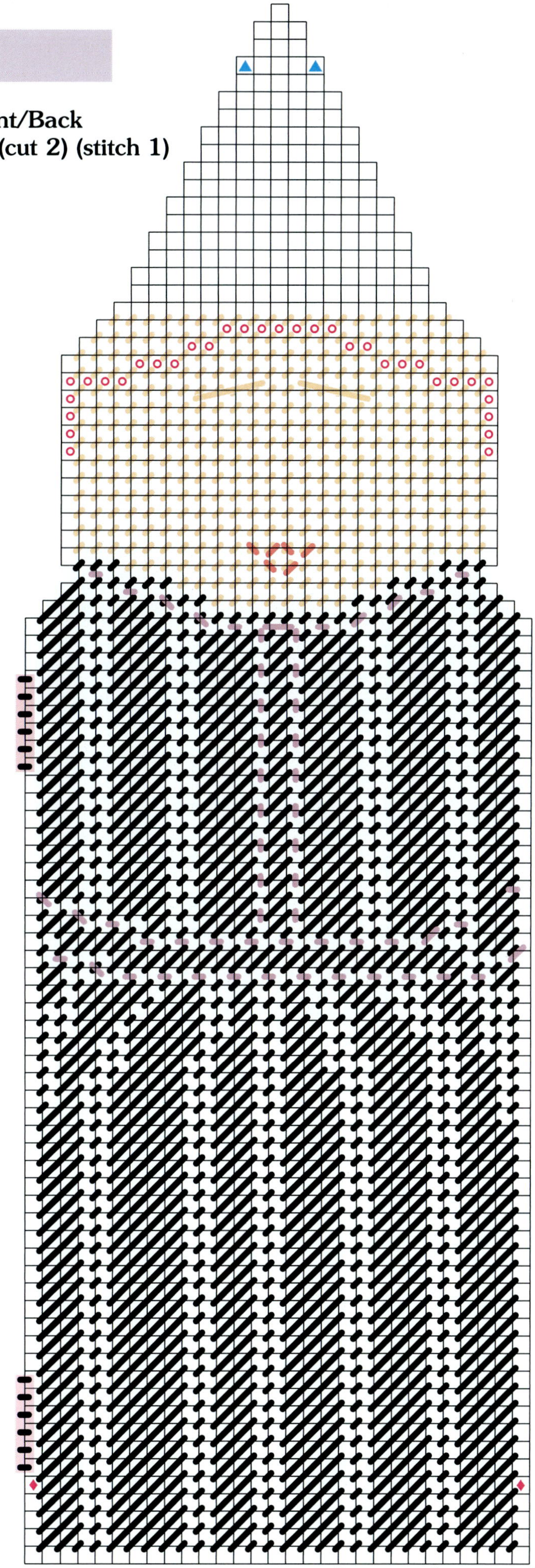

Frog (11 x 11 threads)

Witch Arms
(30 x 20 threads)

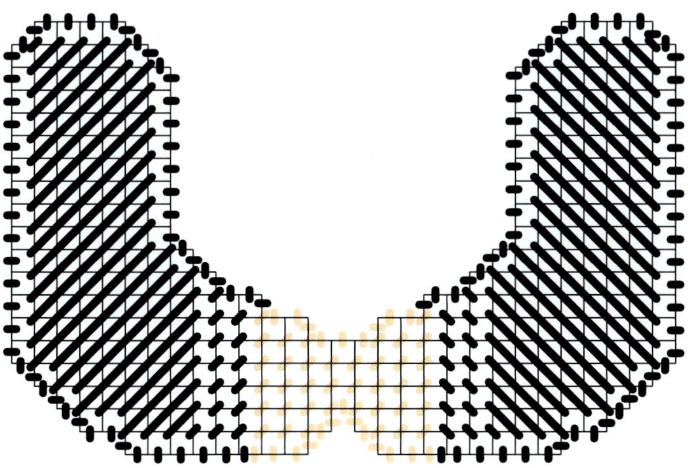

Witch Shoes
(30 x 10 threads)

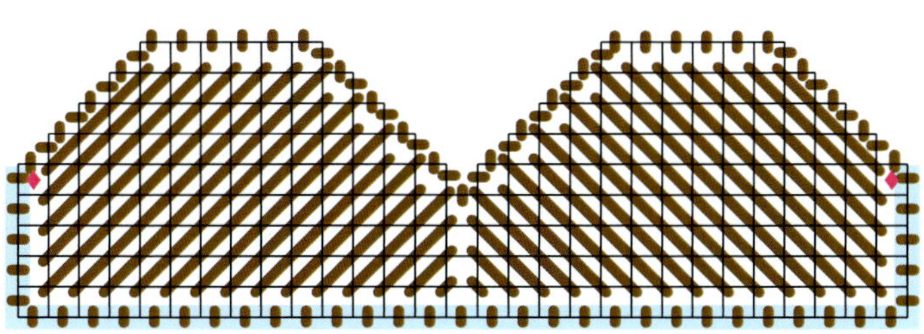

Continued on pg. 10.

THANKSGIVING

Size: 23½"w x 13½"h
Supplies: Worsted weight yarn (refer to color keys), seven 10½" x 13½" sheets of clear 7 mesh plastic canvas, #16 tapestry needle, two 3" x 7½" white foam board rectangles, three 3" x 10" white foam board rectangles, six 12mm moveable eyes, powder blush, and craft glue.
Instructions:
You will need to refer to the photo when assembling your Thanksgiving Lineup. Follow charts to cut and stitch Thanksgiving pieces, working backstitches, French knots, and Turkey loops last and leaving shaded areas unworked.

Pumpkins
1. Twist and tack Vines to Pumpkin Fronts. Tack Stems and Leaves to Pumpkin Fronts.
2. Placing 3" x 7½" foam board rectangle between Pumpkin Front and Back, use dk orange overcast stitches to join unshaded edges of Pumpkin Front and Back. Repeat for second Pumpkin.

Indian
1. Tack Headband, Nose, and Arms to Indian Front. Glue eyes to Indian Front.
2. Matching ★'s, tack top of Shoes to Indian Front. Working stitches in blue shaded area and stitching through three layers of canvas, join Shoes to Indian Front and Back.
3. Placing 3" x 10" foam board rectangle between Indian Front and Back, refer to photo for yarn colors and use overcast stitches to join unshaded edges of Indian Front and Back.
4. For each braid, cut seven 10" lengths of black yarn. Fold yarn in half and braid. Tie 4" length of black yarn around braid end to secure braid; trim ends. Tack braids to Indian.
5. For fringe on shirt, trim Turkey loops as desired and separate yarn plies.

Pilgrim Boy
1. Tack Buckle to Hat Brim. Tack Hat Brim to Boy Front. Tack Nose, Left and Right Collars, and Arms to Boy Front. Glue eyes to Boy Front.
2. Matching ♥'s, tack top of Shoes to Boy Front. Working stitches in yellow shaded area and stitching through three layers of canvas, join Shoes to Boy Front and Back.
3. Placing 3" x 10" foam board rectangle between Boy Front and Back, refer to photo for yarn colors and use overcast stitches to join unshaded edges of Boy Front and Back.
4. Apply blush to Boy's face.
5. Tack Beak to Turkey Body. Tack Turkey Legs and Feathers to wrong side of Turkey Body. Tack Turkey Back to wrong side of Feathers and Turkey Body. Tack Turkey to Boy.

Pilgrim Girl
1. Tack Pie to Arms. Tack Nose, Apron, Lace, and Arms to Girl Front. Glue eyes to Girl Front.
2. Matching ■'s, work stitches in blue shaded area to join Hat Brim to Hat. Matching ▲'s and stitching through three layers of canvas, work stitches in green shaded area to join Hat to Girl Front and Back.
3. Placing 3" x 10" foam board rectangle between Girl Front and Back, use matching color overcast stitches to join unshaded edges of Girl Front and Back.
4. Apply blush to Girl's face.

Joining the Lineup
Work stitches in pink shaded areas to cover unworked edges of Fronts only. Insert Hinges in openings on pie sides. Work stitches in grey shaded areas to join Hinges to unworked edges of Backs only.

Stem
(8 x 9 threads) (stitch 2)

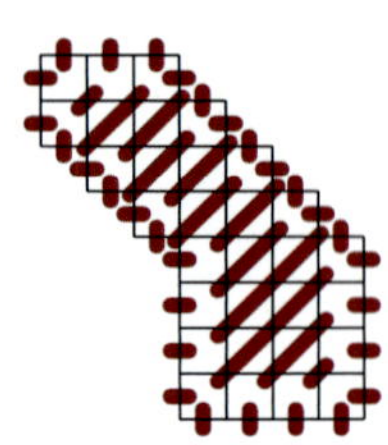

Hinge
(14 x 7 threads) (stitch 8)

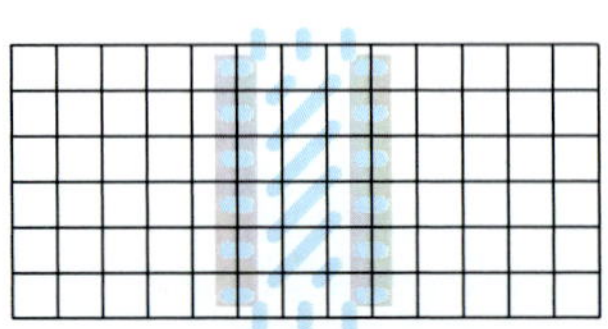

Pumpkin Leaf
(8 x 7 threads) (stitch 4)

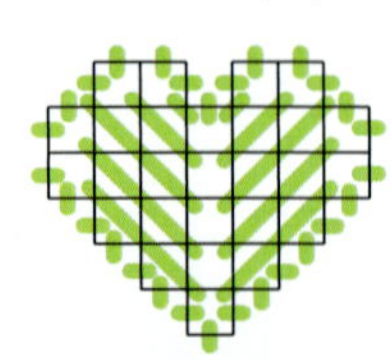

KEY

COLOR
orange
dk orange
green
dk brown
grey

Vine
(2 x 45 threads) (stitch 2)

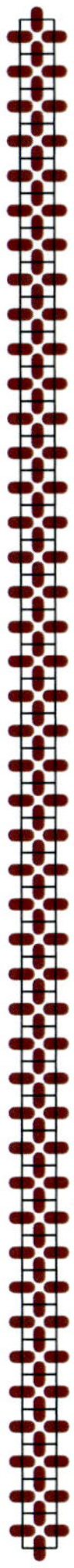

Pumpkin Front/Back
(30 x 60 threads) (cut 4) (stitch 2)

Continued on pg. 12.

Indian Front/Back
(30 x 81 threads) (cut 2) (stitch 1)

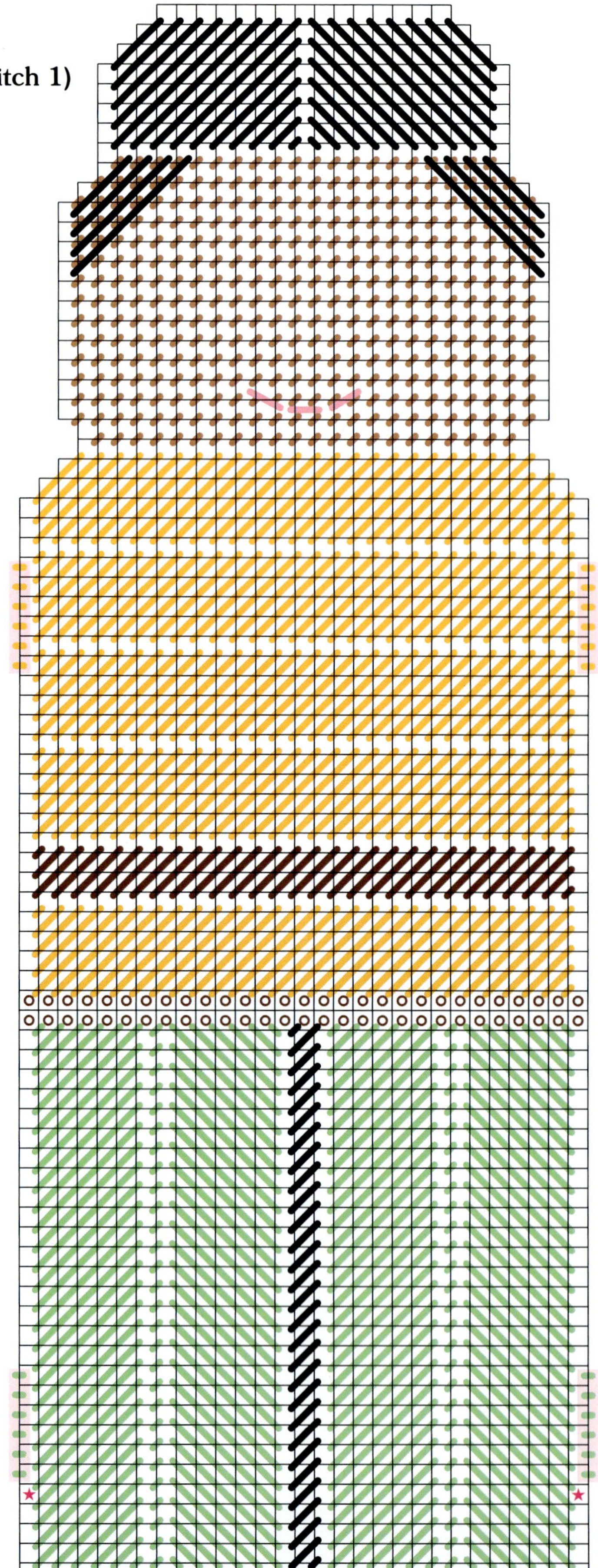

Indian Nose
(4 x 4 threads) (cut 2)
Stack and stitch through two layers of canvas.

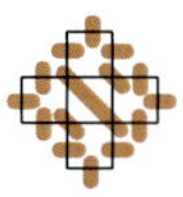

Headband (22 x 6 threads)

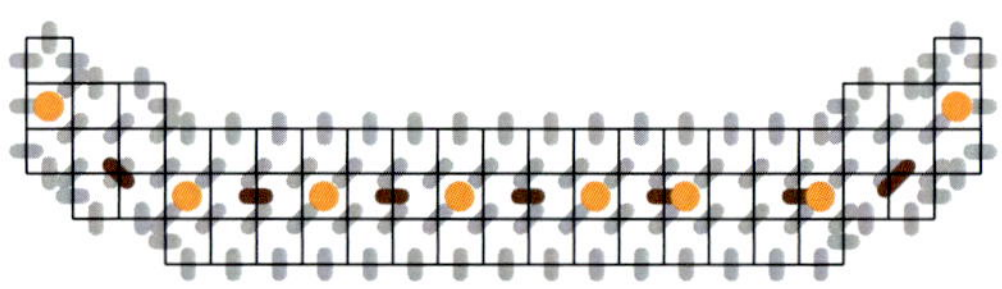

Indian Arms
(30 x 20 threads)

Indian Shoes
(30 x 10 threads)

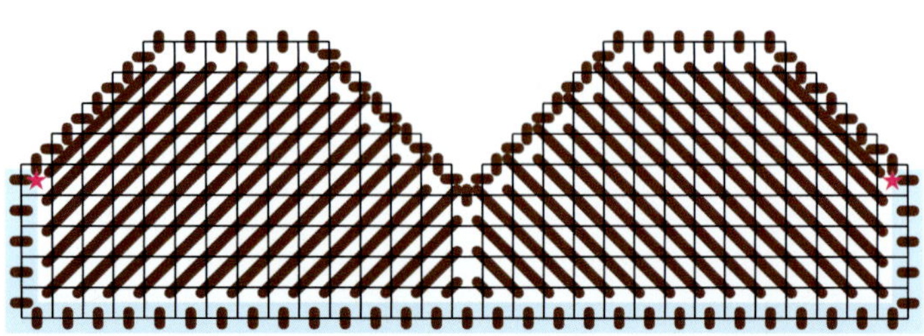

KEY

COLOR
white
lt yellow
yellow
gold
dk orange
rose
dk red
brown
dk brown
black
orange Fr. knot
dk red Fr. knot
black Fr. knot
dk brown Turkey loop

Turkey Back
(16 x 19 threads)

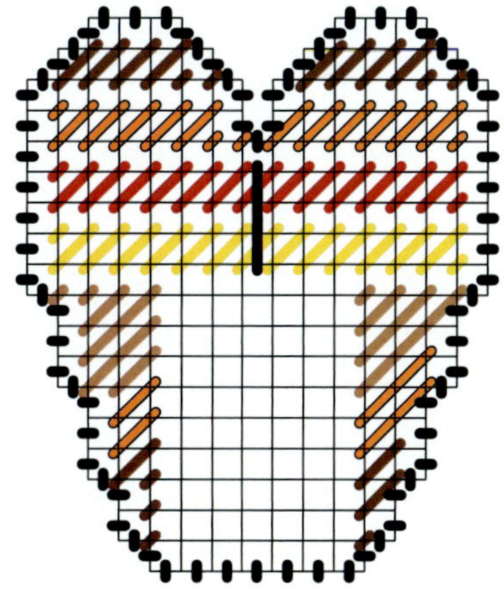

Turkey Body
(15 x 22 threads)

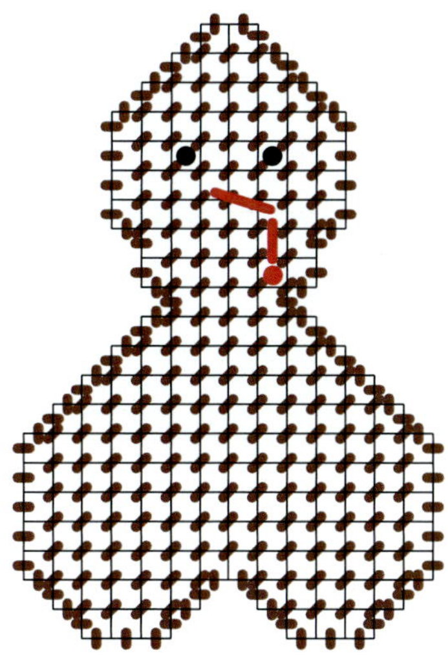

Beak
(4 x 4 threads)

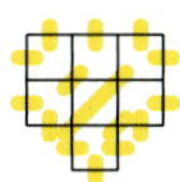

Feathers
(8 x 16 threads) (stitch 4)

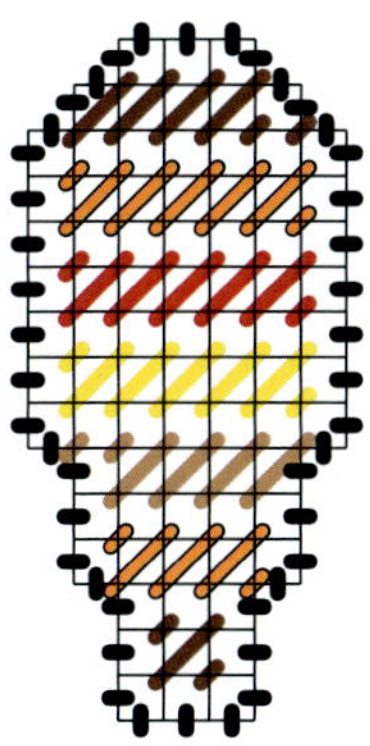

Left Leg
(5 x 13 threads)

Right Leg
(5 x 13 threads)

Continued on pg. 14.

KEY

COLOR	COLOR
white	dk grey
yellow	black
flesh	*brown
rose	*Use two strands of yarn.
brown	

Boy Nose
(4 x 4 threads) (cut 2)
Stack and stitch through two layers of canvas.

Left Collar (11 x 8 threads)

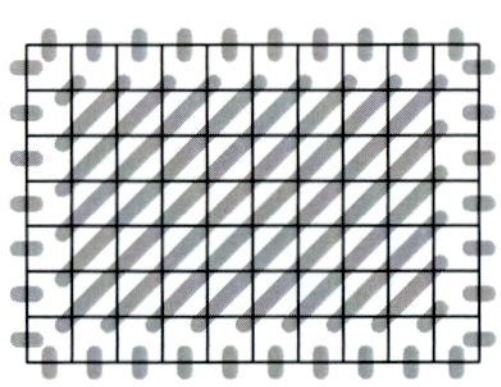

Right Collar (11 x 8 threads)

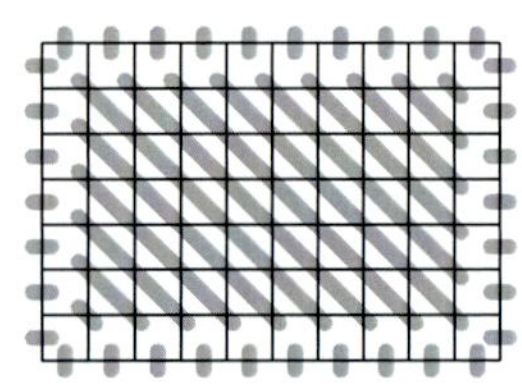

Boy Hat Brim
(30 x 7 threads)

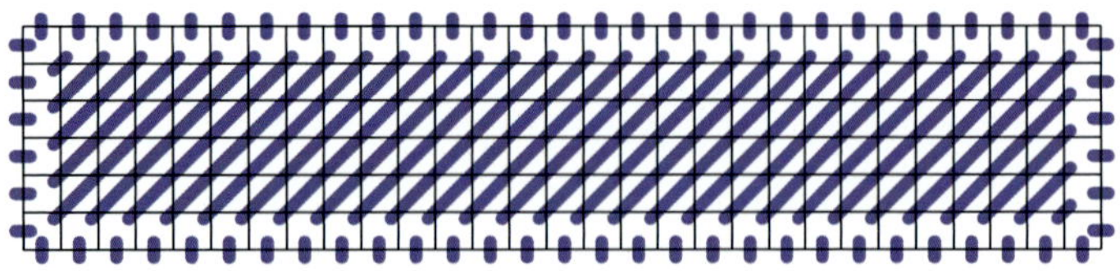

Buckle (8 x 8 threads)

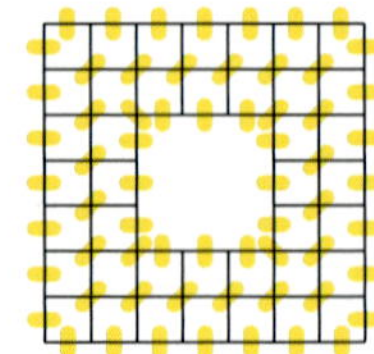

Boy Front/Back
(30 x 90 threads) (cut 2) (stitch 1)

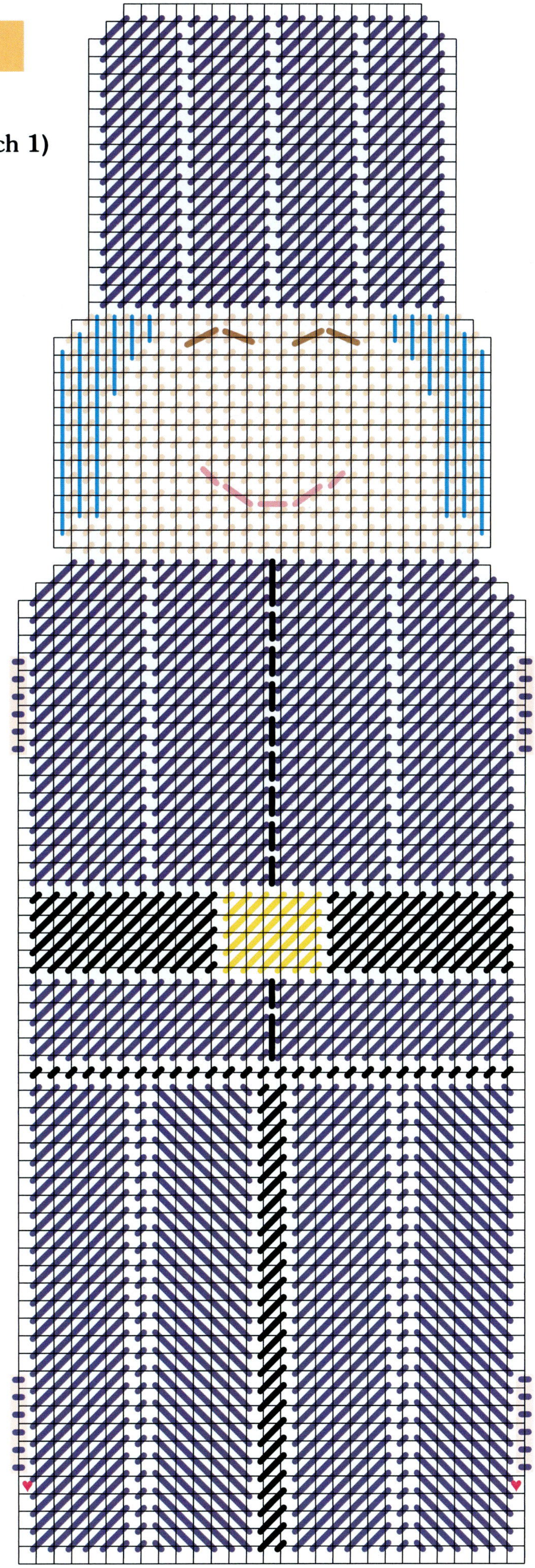

Boy Arms
(30 x 20 threads)

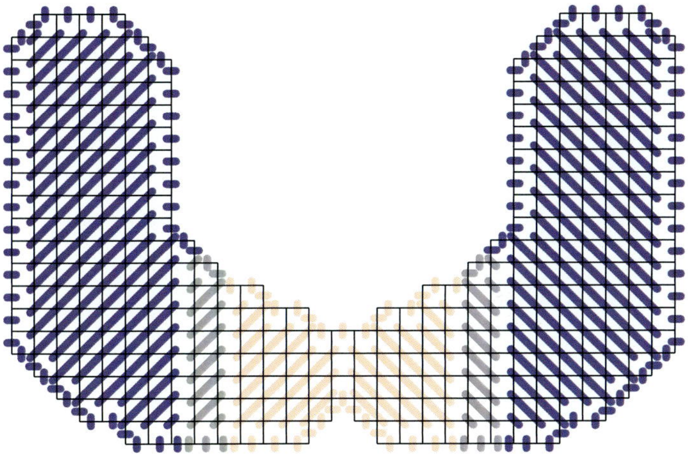

Boy Shoes
(30 x 10 threads)

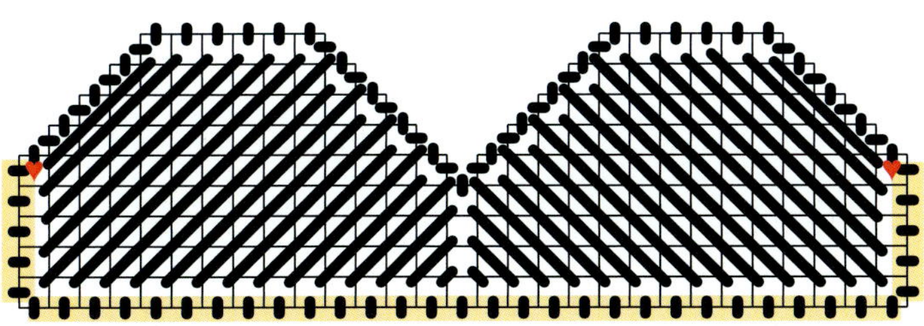

Continued on pg. 16.

KEY

COLOR	COLOR
white	brown
flesh	lt grey
rose	dk grey
dk red	brown Turkey loop

Girl Hat (22 x 19 threads)

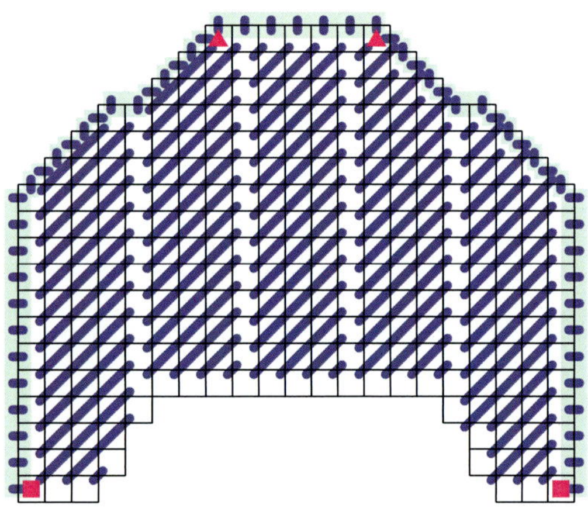

Girl Apron
(30 x 46 threads)

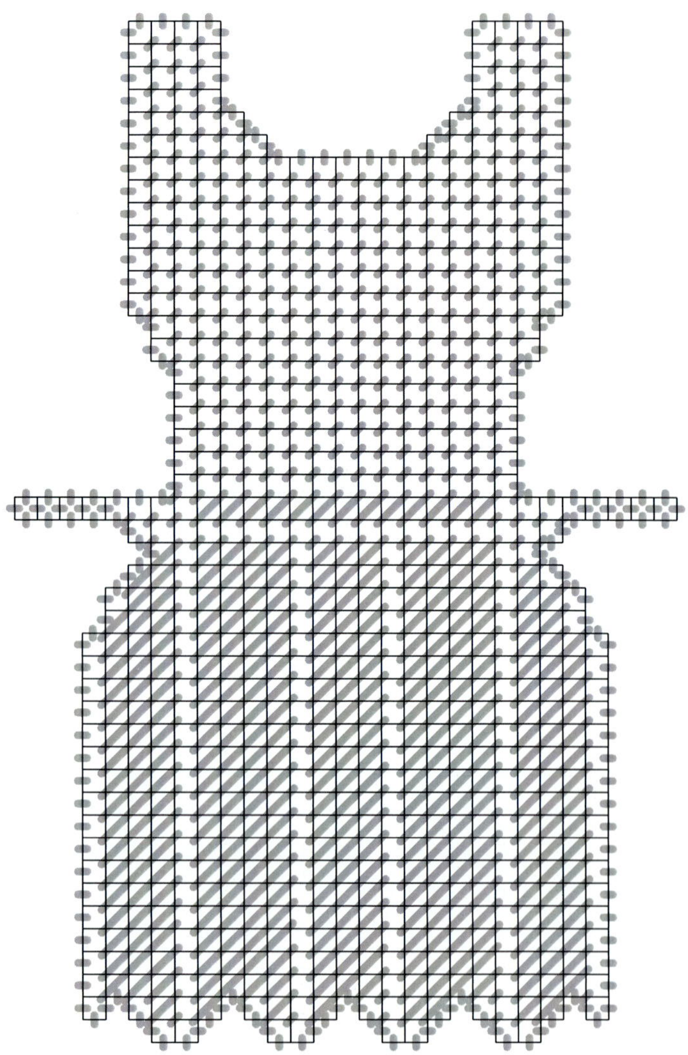

Girl Hat Brim
(30 x 11 threads)

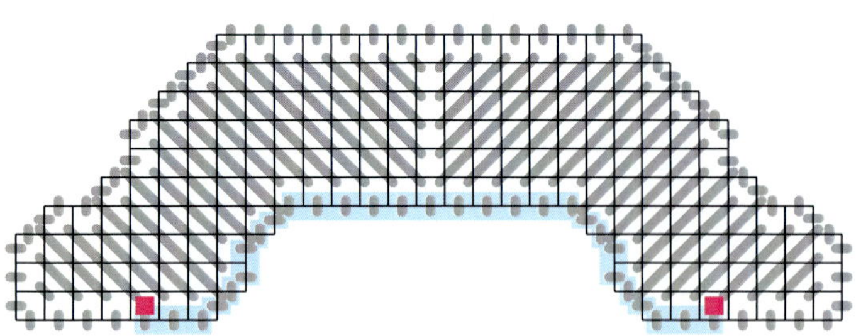

Girl Front/Back
(30 x 88 threads) (cut 2) (stitch 1)

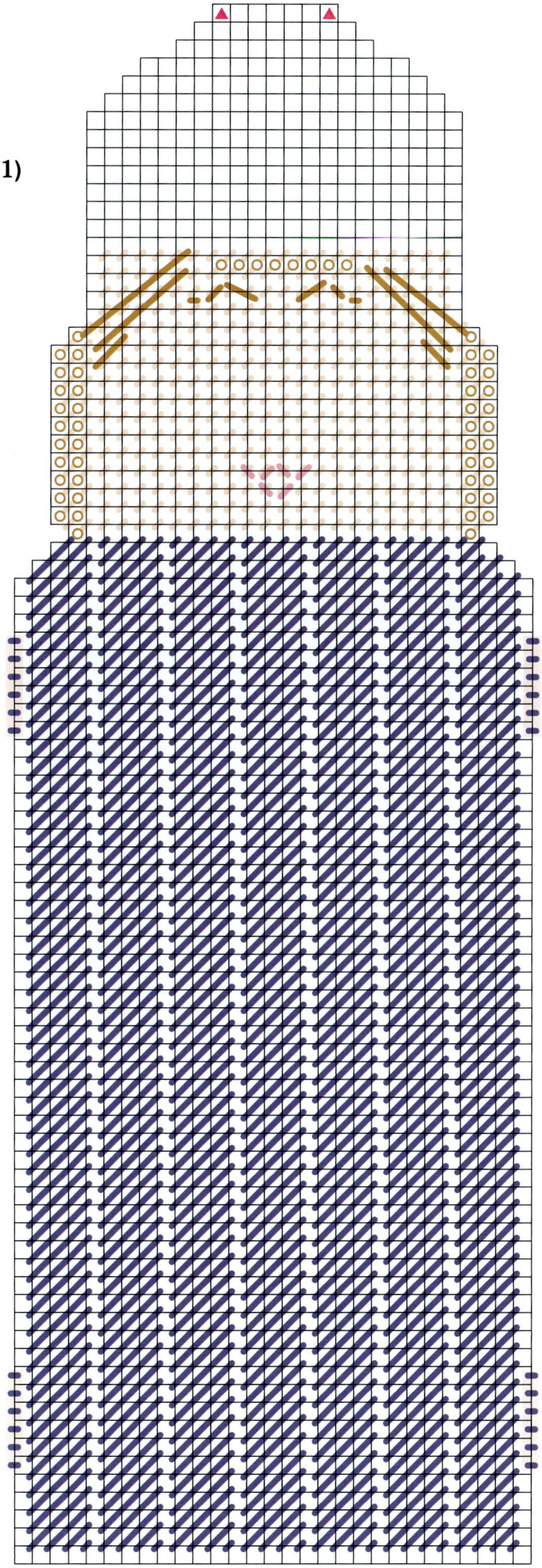

Girl Nose
(4 x 4 threads) (cut 2)
Stack and stitch through two layers of canvas.

Pie (15 x 10 threads)

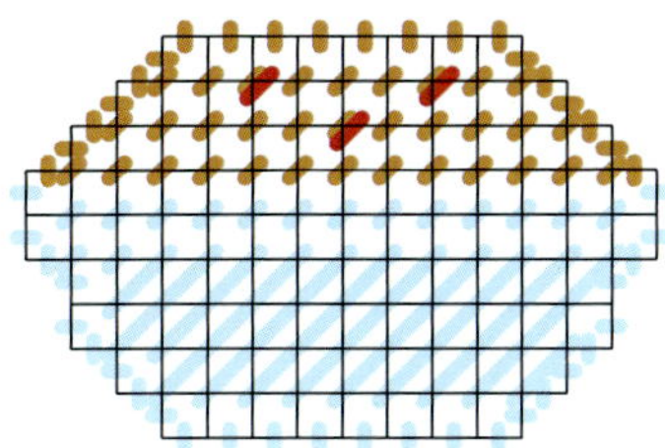

Girl Arms
(30 x 20 threads)

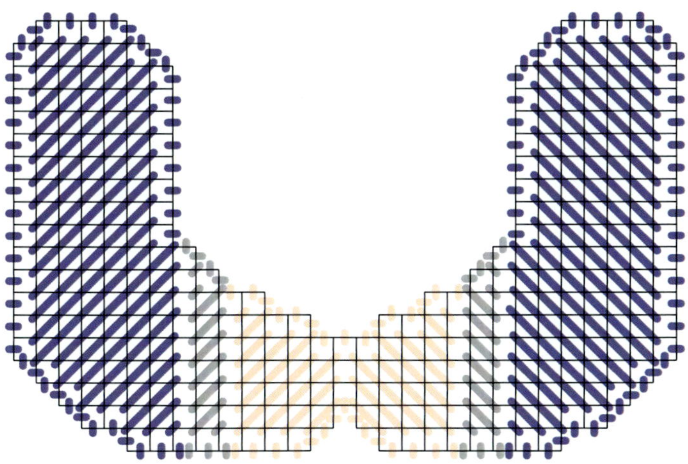

Girl Lace
(30 x 5 threads)

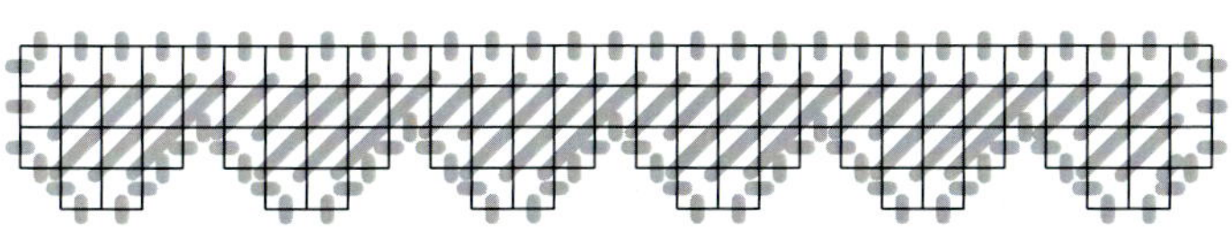

Continued on pg. 20.

CHRISTMAS

Size: 19"w x 15"h
Supplies: Worsted weight yarn (refer to color keys), six 10½" x 13½" sheets of clear 7 mesh plastic canvas, #16 tapestry needle, four 3" x 10" white foam board rectangles, six 12mm moveable eyes, one ½" jingle bell, six red buttons, 17" length metallic gold ribbon, three ¼" jingle bells, four 6mm gold beads, powder blush, and craft glue.
Instructions:
You will need to refer to the photo when assembling your Christmas Lineup. Follow charts to cut and stitch Christmas pieces, working backstitches and French knots last and leaving shaded areas unworked.

Reindeer

1. Tack Large Heart, Bow, and Head to Reindeer Front. Cut a 12" length of dk green yarn. Thread yarn through ½" jingle bell. Insert both ends of yarn through Reindeer Head from front to back. Insert both ends of yarn back through Reindeer Head from back to front. Tie bow; trim ends.
2. Placing foam board rectangle between Reindeer Front and Back, use matching color overcast stitches to join unshaded edges of Reindeer Front and Back.

Santa

1. Tack Nose and top edge of Mustache to Santa Front. Glue eyes to Santa Front.
2. Glue buttons to Wreath. Cut a 9" length of red yarn. Tie bow and glue bow to Wreath. Insert Arms through Wreath. Tack Arms and Wreath to Santa Front.
3. Matching ★'s, tack bottom edge of Hat to Santa Front. Working stitches in yellow shaded area and stitching through three layers of canvas, join Hat to Santa Front and Back. Glue Eyebrows to Hat and Santa Front. Tack Pom-pom to Hat.
4. Matching ♥'s, work stitches in green shaded areas through three layers of canvas to join Beard to Santa Front and Back.
5. Matching ▲'s, tack top of Shoes to Santa Front. Place foam board rectangle between Santa Front and Back. Working stitches in blue shaded area and stitching through three layers of canvas, join Shoes to Santa Front and Back. Using matching color overcast stitches, join unshaded edges of Santa Front and Back.
6. Apply blush to Santa's face.

Mrs. Santa

1. Tack Nose and Lace to Mrs. Santa Front. Tack Small Heart to Apron; tack Apron to Mrs. Santa Front. Tack Leaves to Hat Brim; tack Hat Brim to Mrs. Santa Front. Tack Cookies to Cookie Sheet; tack Cookie Sheet to Arms; tack Arms to Apron and Mrs. Santa Front. Glue eyes to Mrs. Santa Front.
2. Placing foam board rectangle between Mrs. Santa Front and Back, use matching color overcast stitches to join unshaded edges of Mrs. Santa Front and Back.
3. Apply blush to Mrs. Santa's face.

Elf

1. Tack Nose and Ears to Elf Front. Glue eyes to Elf Front. Tack beads to Elf Front.
2. Using bright green overcast stitches, join Box Sides along short edges. Join Box Top and Bottom to Sides along long edges. Tack Box to wrong side of Arms. Tack Arms to Elf Front. Tie bow with ribbon; glue ribbon to Box, Arms, and Elf Front.
3. Turn Shoes over. Referring to Elf Shoes Diagram, work stitches in blue shaded areas on "wrong side" of Shoes. Turn piece to the "right side" and tack tips of Shoes to the front of the Shoes. Tack ¼" jingle bells to tips.
4. Matching ■'s, tack top of Shoes to Elf Front. Place 3" x 10" foam board rectangle between Elf Front and Back. Working stitches in yellow shaded area and stitching through three layers of canvas, join Shoes to Elf Front and Back. Referring to photo for yarn colors, use overcast stitches to join unshaded edges of Elf Front and Back.
5. Tack ¼" jingle bell to tip of hat.
6. Apply blush to Elf's face.

Joining the Lineup

Work stitches in pink shaded areas to cover unworked edges of Fronts only. Insert Hinges in openings on piece sides. Work stitches in grey shaded areas to join Hinges to unworked edges of Backs only.

Bow
(17 x 10 threads)

Hinge
(14 x 7 threads) (stitch 6)

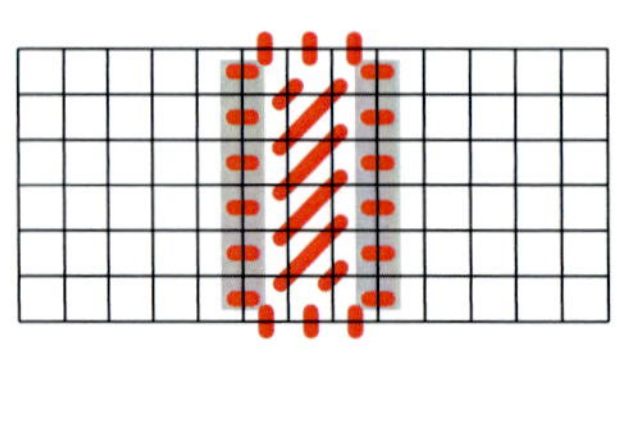

Large Heart
(12 x 12 threads)

KEY

	COLOR
	red
	green
	dk green
	tan
	brown
	black
	red Fr. knot

Reindeer Head
(30 x 55 threads)

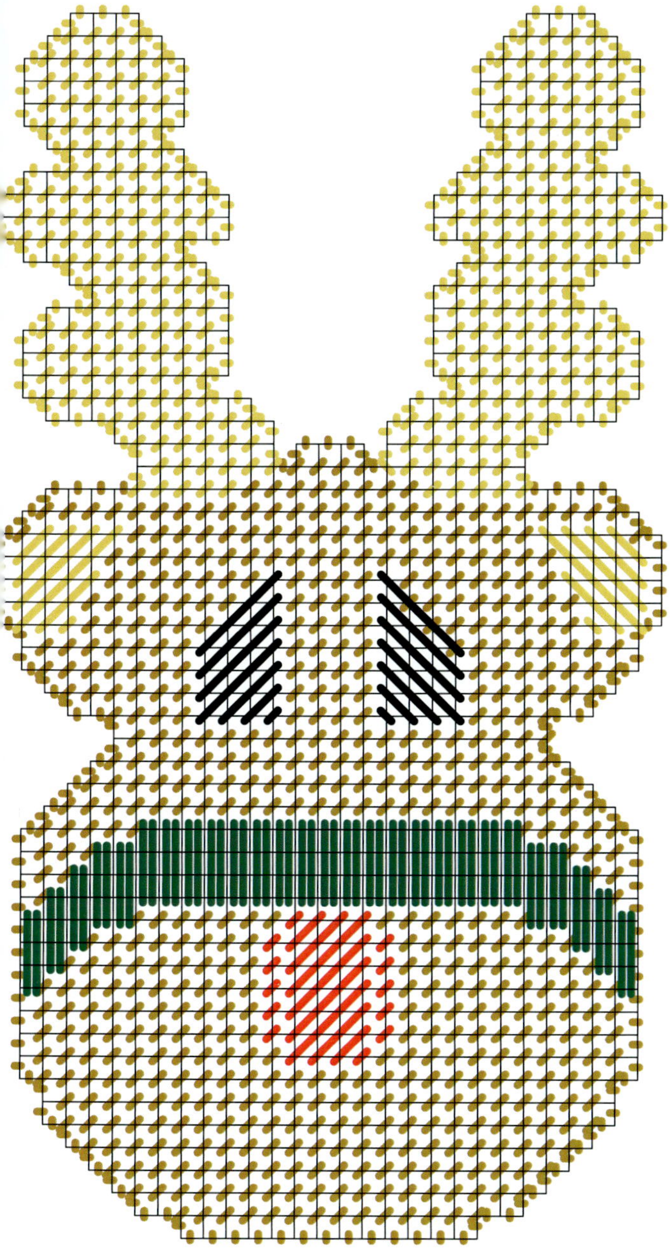

Reindeer Front/Back
(30 x 78 threads) (cut 2) (stitch 1)

Continued on pg. 22.

Santa Eyebrow
(4 x 4 threads)

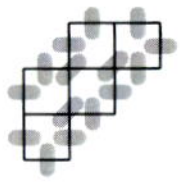

Santa Eyebrow
(4 x 4 threads)

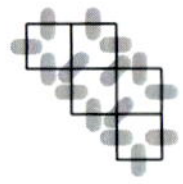

Santa Nose
(4 x 4 threads) (cut 2)
Stack and stitch through two layers of canvas.

Pom-pom
(8 x 8 threads)

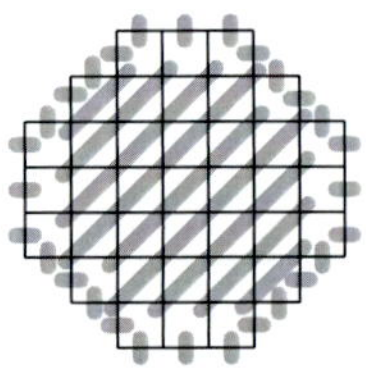

Mustache
(13 x 4 threads)

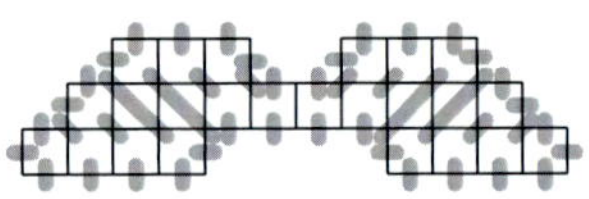

Santa Hat
(27 x 19 threads)

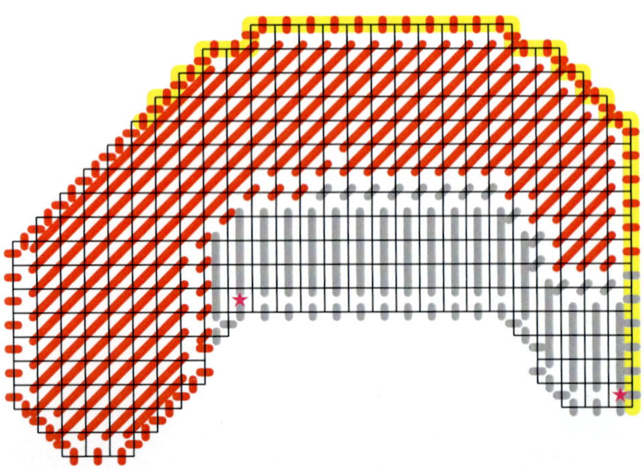

Beard
(26 x 13 threads)
After working overcast stitches, refer to Diagram and tie 4" lengths of white yarn to threads to cover Beard. Trim ends.

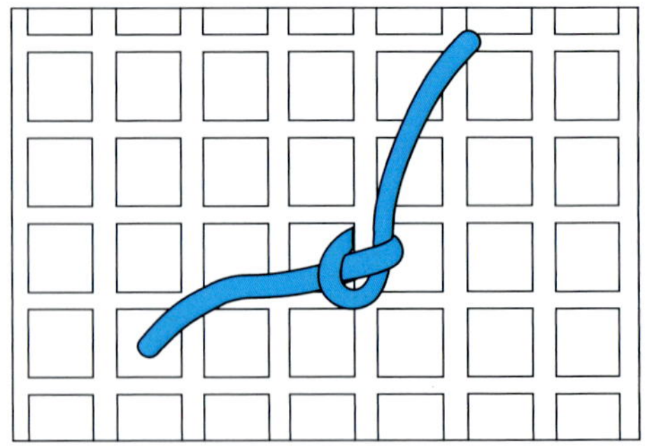

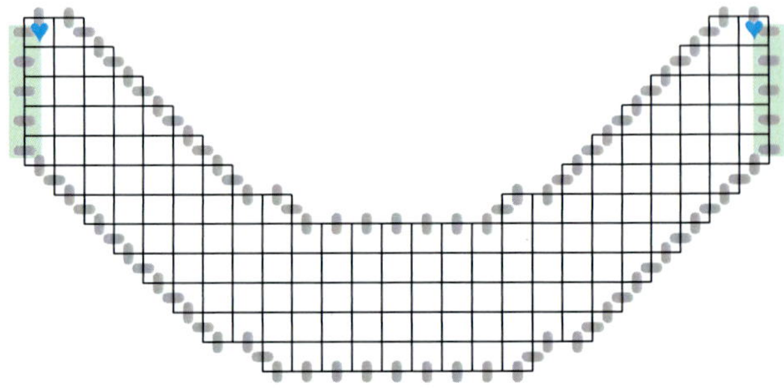

Wreath
(24 x 24 threads)

Santa Front/Back
(30 x 89 threads) (cut 2) (stitch 1)

KEY

COLOR
white
flesh
pink
red
green
black

Santa Arms
(30 x 23 threads)

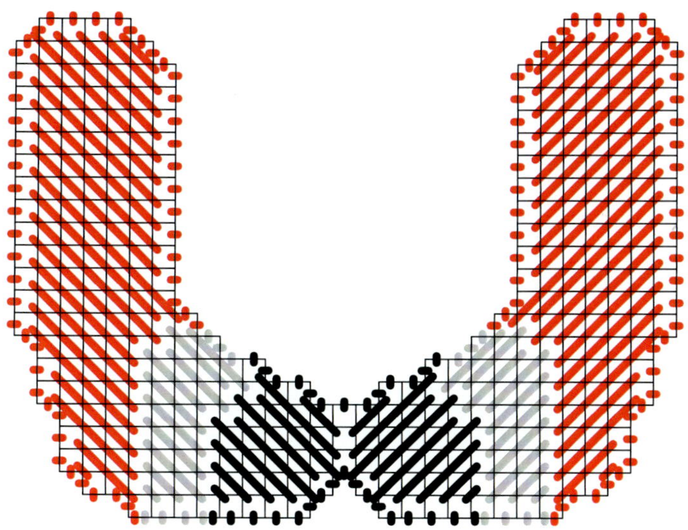

Santa Shoes
(30 x 10 threads)

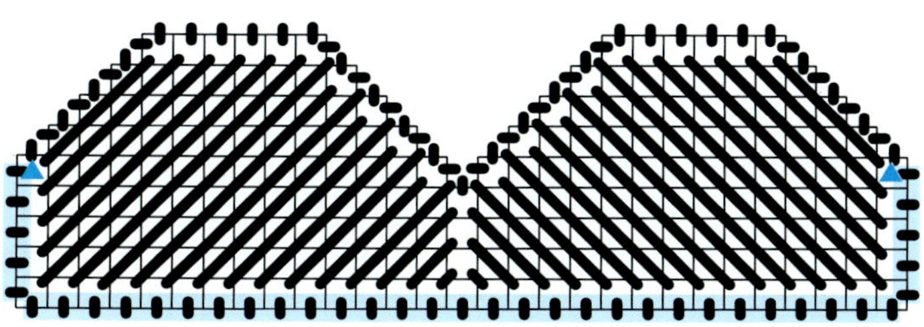

Continued on pg. 24.

Mrs. Santa Nose
(4 x 4 threads) (cut 2)
Stack and stitch through two layers of canvas.

Mrs. Santa Leaf
(4 x 6 threads) (stitch 2)

Mrs. Santa Hat Brim
(28 x 11 threads)

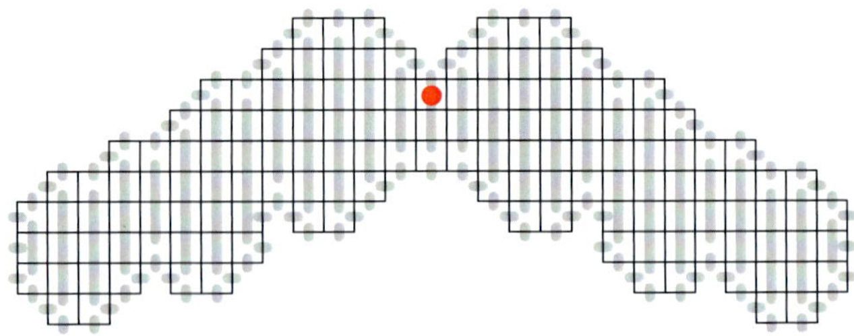

Small Heart
(8 x 7 threads)

Mrs. Santa Apron
(30 x 46 threads)

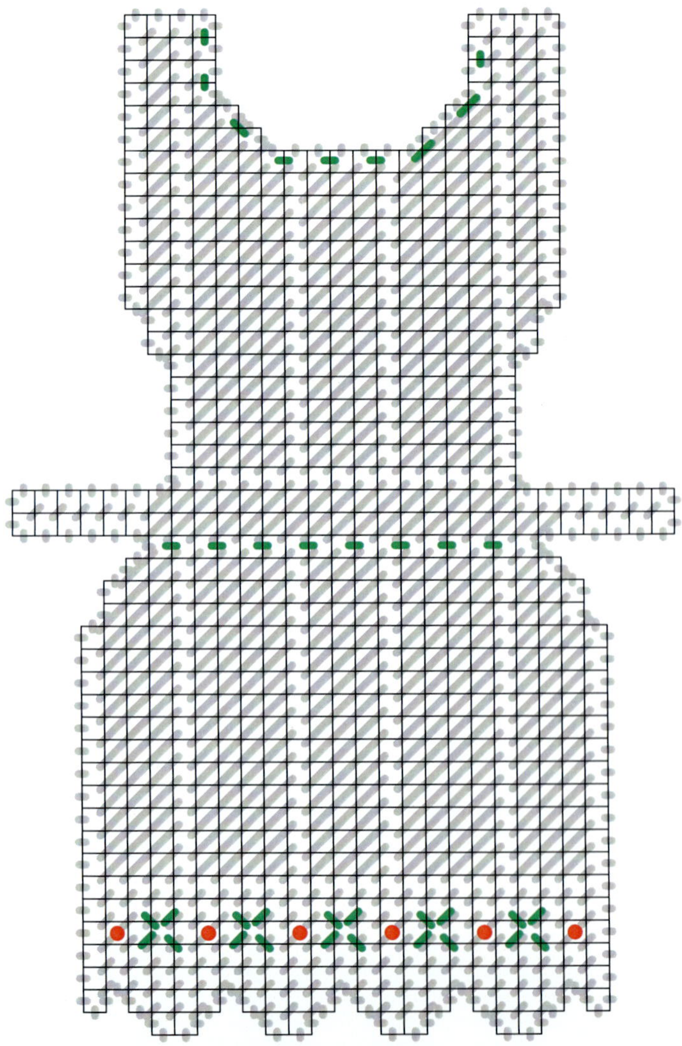

Girl Cookie
(7 x 10 threads)

Boy Cookie
(7 x 10 threads)

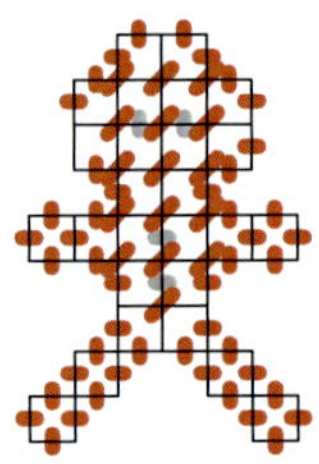

Cookie Sheet
(17 x 12 threads)

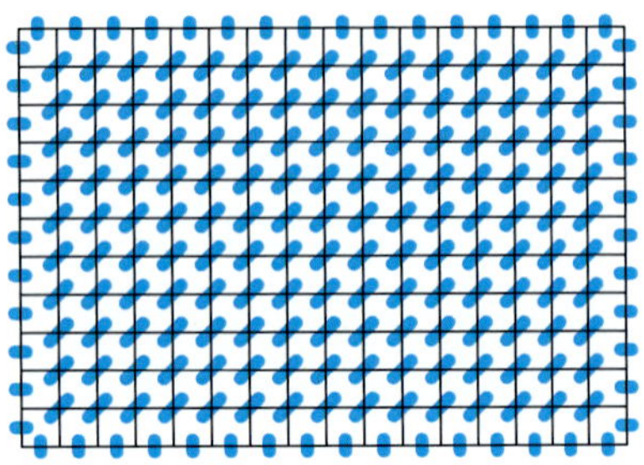

Mrs. Santa Front/Back
(30 x 85 threads) (cut 2) (stitch 1)

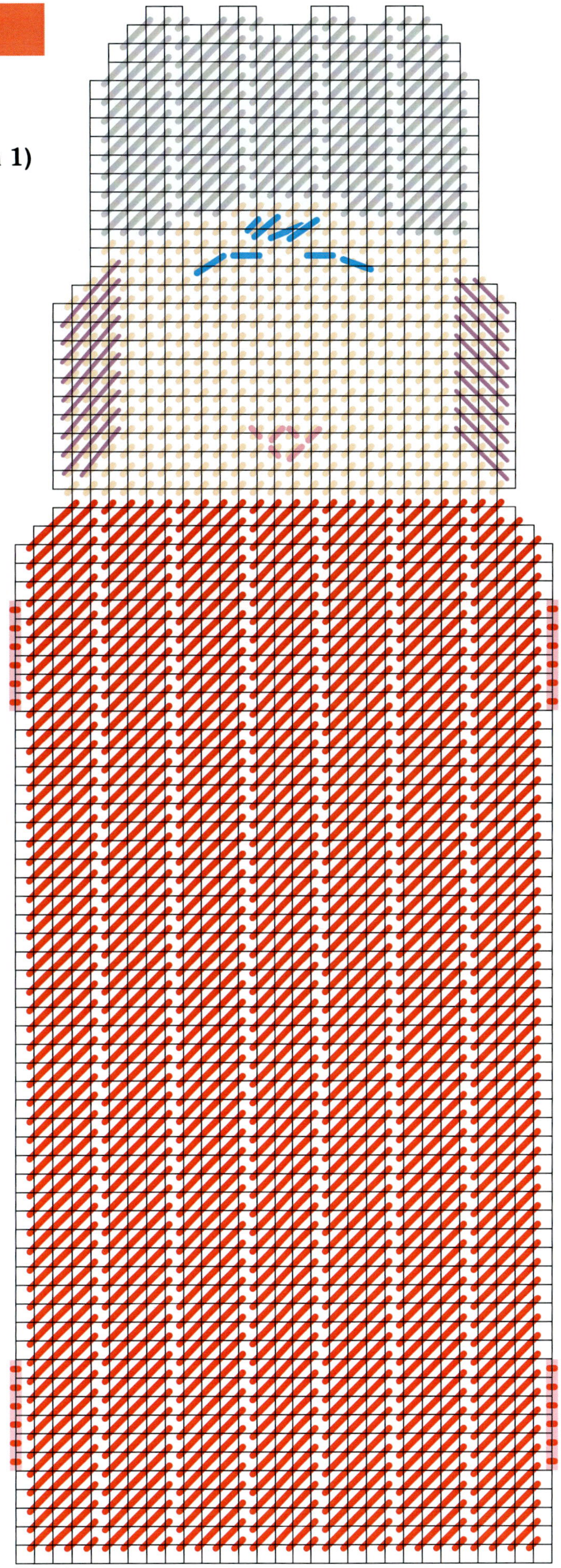

KEY

	COLOR
white	white
flesh	flesh
rose	rose
red	red
green	green
dk brown	dk brown
lt grey	lt grey
*lt grey	*lt grey
red Fr. knot	red Fr. knot

*Use 2 strands of yarn.

Mrs. Santa Arms
(30 x 20 threads)

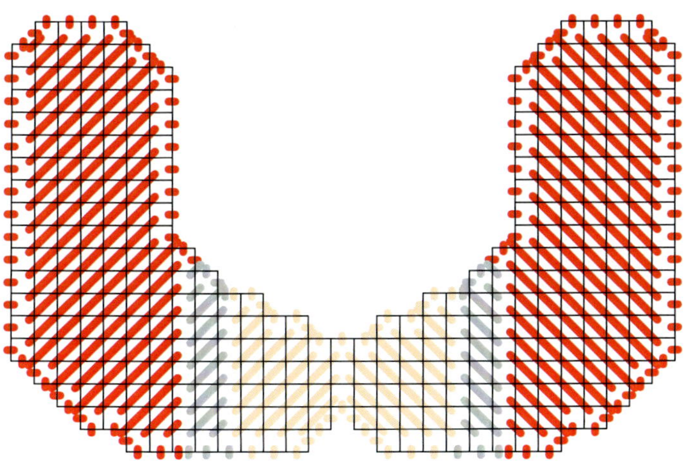

Mrs. Santa Lace
(30 x 5 threads)

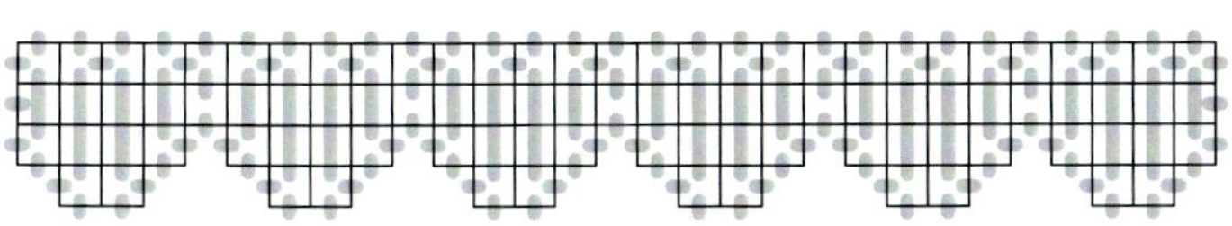

Continued on pg. 26.

KEY

COLOR
white
flesh
rose
red
dk red
bright green
dk green
brown
dk brown
black

Elf Nose
(4 x 4 threads) (cut 2)
Stack and stitch through two layers of canvas.

Box Side
(3 x 9 threads) (stitch 4)

Box Top/Bottom
(9 x 9 threads) (stitch 2)

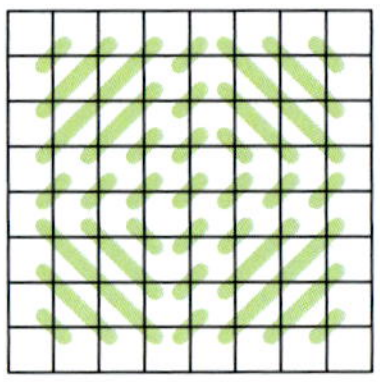

Elf Arms
(30 x 20 threads)

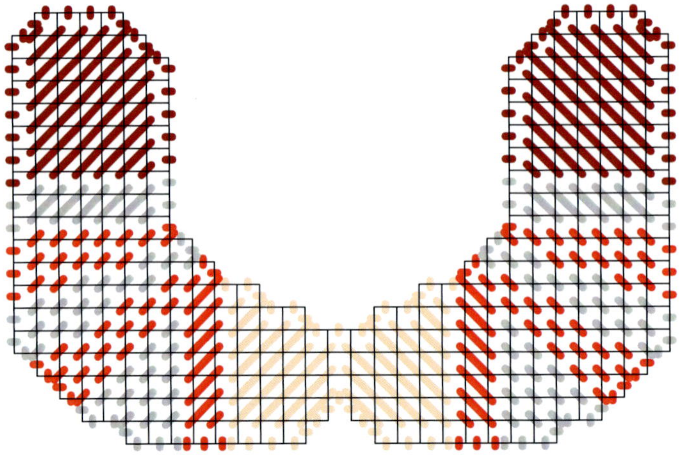

Elf Front/Back
(30 x 86 threads) (cut 2) (stitch 1)

Elf Left Ear
(4 x 7 threads)

Elf Right Ear
(4 x 7 threads)

Elf Shoes Diagram

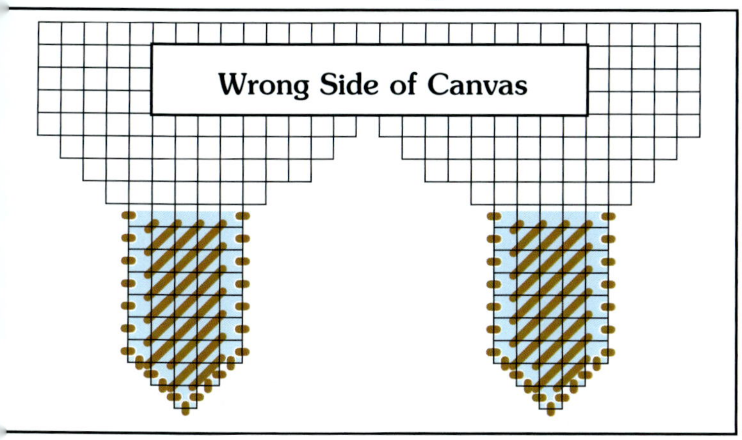

Elf Shoes
(30 x 18 threads)

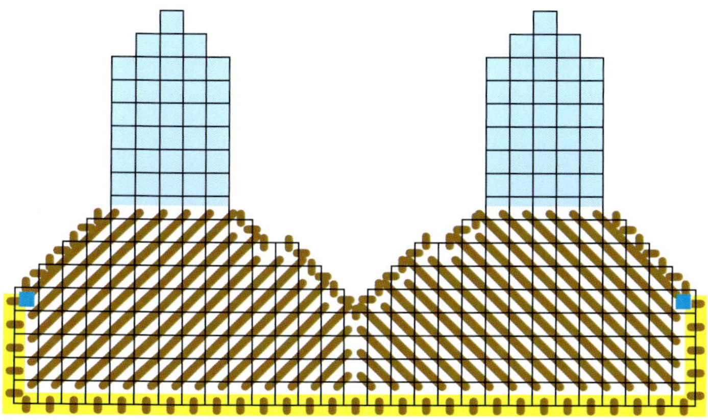

SNOW FAMILY

Size: 20"w x 14"h
Supplies: Worsted weight (refer to color keys), six $10^1/_2$" x $13^1/_2$" sheets of clear 7 mesh plastic canvas, #16 tapestry needle, four 3" x 10" white foam board rectangles, thirteen assorted buttons, three pink silk ribbon roses, 7" length of pre-strung pearls, cardboard, and craft glue.
Instructions:
You will need to refer to the photo when assembling your Snow Family Lineup. Follow charts to cut and stitch Snow Family pieces, working backstitches, French knots, and fringe stitches last and leaving shaded areas unworked.

Stocking Cap Snowman

1. Tack Eyes, edge of Nose, and Large Heart to Stocking Cap Snowman Front. Tack Scarf Tail to Scarf; tack Scarf to Stocking Cap Snowman Front. Tack Wing and Beak to Blue Bird; tack Blue Bird to Stocking Cap Snowman Front. Glue three buttons to Stocking Cap Snowman Front.
2. Matching ★'s, tack top and bottom edges of Hat Cuff to Stocking Cap Snowman Front. Working stitches in grey shaded areas and stitching through three layers of canvas, join Hat Cuff to Stocking Cap Snowman Front and Back.
3. Placing foam board rectangle between Stocking Cap Snowman Front and Back, use matching color overcast stitches to join unshaded edges of Stocking Cap Snowman Front and Back.
4. To make a pom-pom for the stocking cap, cut a 4" x 3" cardboard rectangle. Cut a 5" length of red yarn. Referring to Diagram A, wrap three yards each of blue and red yarn around cardboard. Remove cardboard from yarn circle. Referring to Diagram B, tie 5" length of yarn around center of yarn circle. Clip loops of yarn circle. Trim ends to shape.
5. Tack pom-pom to stocking cap.

Snowlady

1. Tack Eyes and edge of Nose to Snowlady Front. Glue ribbon roses to Earmuffs and Snowlady Front. Glue three buttons to Snowlady Front.
2. Placing foam board rectangle between Snowlady Front and Back, use white overcast stitches to join unshaded edges of Snowlady Front and Back.
3. Tack Earmuffs to Snowlady edges.
4. For necklace, glue pearl length in place.

Snowgirl

1. Tack Hat Cuff and edge of Nose to Girl. Tack Scarf Knot to Scarf; tack Scarf to Snowgirl.
2. To make a pom-pom for the Snowgirl's hat, cut a 3" x 2" cardboard rectangle. Cut a 5" length of pink yarn. Referring to Diagram A, wrap three yards of pink yarn around cardboard. Remove cardboard from yarn circle. Referring to Diagram B, tie 5" length of yarn around center of yarn circle. Clip loops of yarn circle. Trim ends to shape.
3. Tack pom-pom to cap.
4. Glue Snowgirl to Snowlady Front.

Top Hat Snowman

1. Tack Eyes and edge of Nose to Top Hat Snowman Front. Tack Star to Hat Brim; tack Star and Hat Brim to Top Hat Snowman Front. Tack Bow to Scarf; tack Scarf to Top Hat Snowman Front. Tack Wing and Beak to Red Bird; tack Red Bird to Top Hat Snowman Front. Glue three buttons to Top Hat Snowman Front.
2. Placing foam board rectangle between Top Hat Snowman Front and Back, use matching color overcast stitches to join unshaded edges of Top Hat Snowman Front and Back.

Vested Snowman

1. Tack Eyes, edge of Nose, and Vest pieces to Vested Snowman Front. Glue two buttons to Vested Snowman Front.
2. Tack Beak and Wing to Little Blue Bird; tack Little Blue Bird and Small Heart to Birdhouse. Cut a 4" length of navy yarn; glue yarn ends to wrong side of Birdhouse. Tack Birdhouse to Vested Snowman Front, looping yarn over button.
3. Matching ■'s, use variegated blue yarn to join Hat Brim to Hat. Matching ♥'s, work stitches in pink shaded area through three layers of canvas to join Hat to Vested Snowman Front and Back.
4. Place 3" x 10" foam board rectangle between Vested Snowman Front and Back. Using matching color overcast stitches to join unshaded edges of Vested Snowman Front and Back.

Joining the Lineup

Work stitches in blue shaded areas to cover unworked edges of Fronts only. Insert Hinges in openings on piece sides. Work stitches in green shaded areas to join Hinges to unworked edges of Backs only.

DIAGRAM A

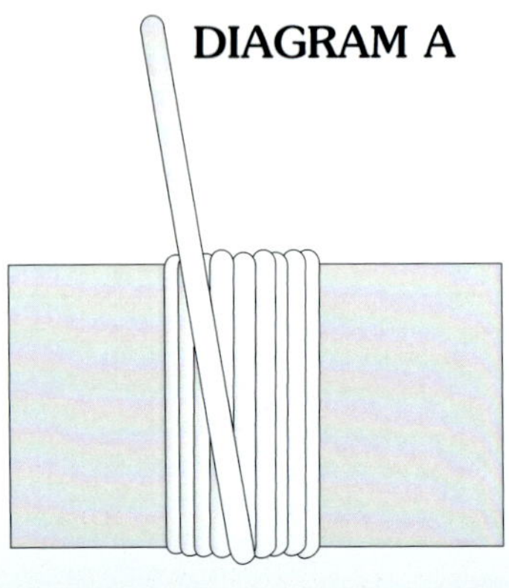

DIAGRAM B

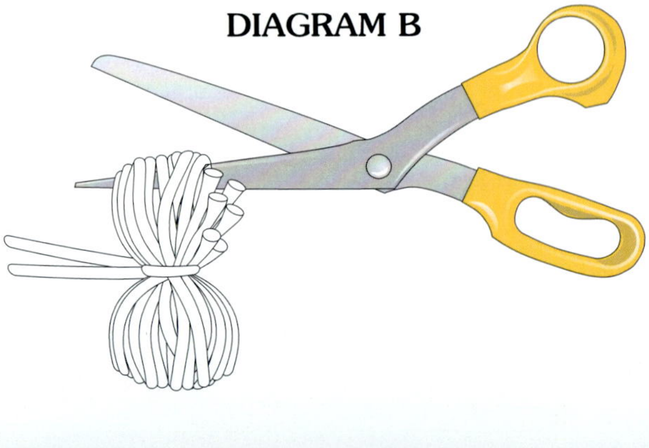

Stocking Cap Snowman Front/Back
(30 x 86 threads) (cut 2) (stitch 1)

KEY

COLOR
white
orange
pink
red
blue
black
black Fr. knot
red fringe
blue fringe

Hinge
(14 x 7 threads) (stitch 6)

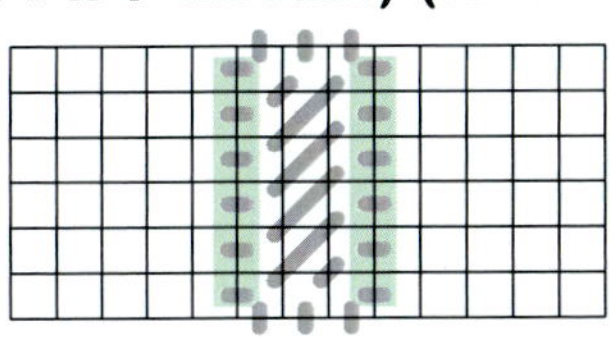

Stocking Cap
Snowman Nose
(7 x 4 threads)

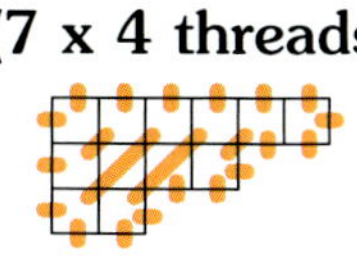

Large Heart
(8 x 8 threads)

Stocking Cap Snowman
Scarf Tail
(15 x 13 threads)

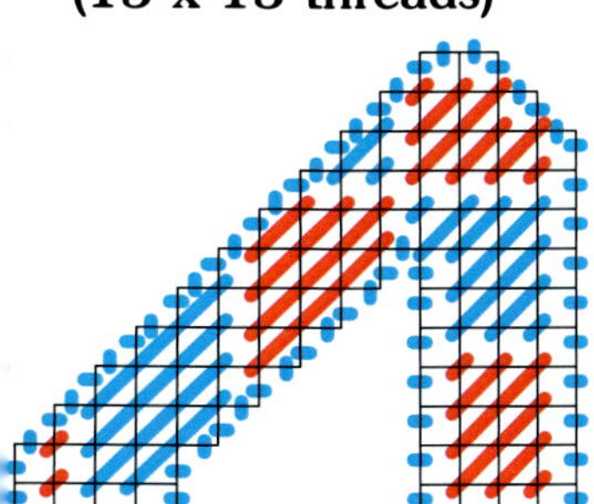

Stocking Cap
Snowman Eye
(4 x 4 threads)
(stitch 2)

Continued on pg. 30.

KEY

COLOR
- white
- yellow
- orange
- pink
- red
- purple
- lt blue
- blue
- grey
- black
- black Fr. knot

Stocking Cap Snowman Scarf
(30 x 9 threads)

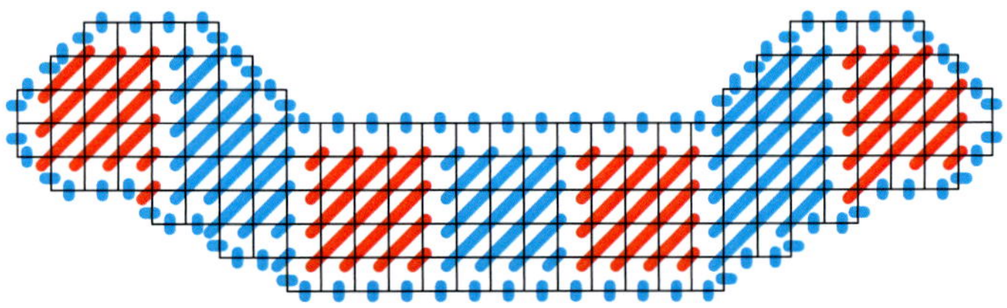

Stocking Cap Snowman Hat Cuff
(30 x 11 threads)

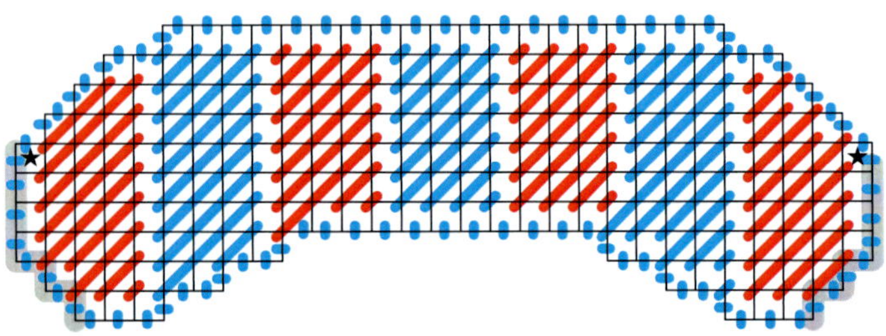

Blue Bird
(17 x 17 threads)

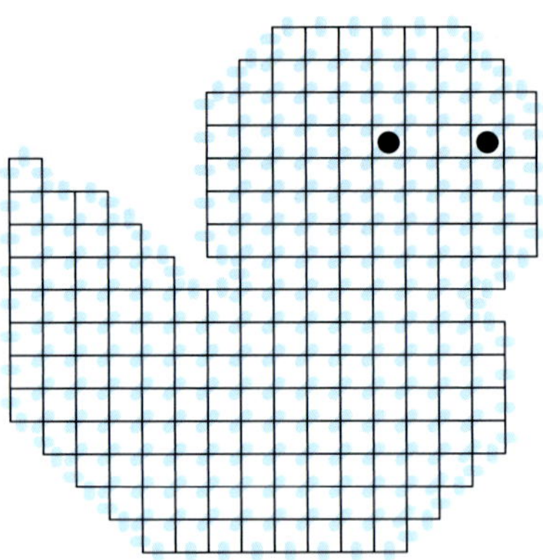

Blue Bird Beak
(4 x 4 threads)

Blue Bird Wing
(11 x 6 threads)

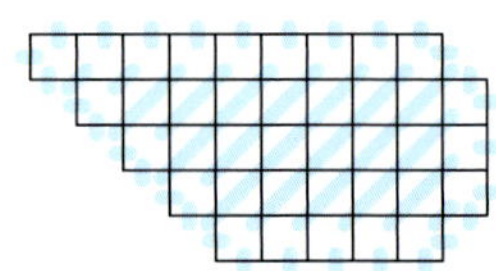

Snowgirl Scarf
(9 x 12 threads)

Snowgirl Scarf Knot
(4 x 4 threads)

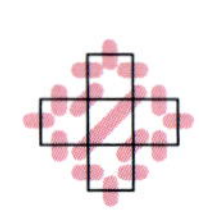

Snowgirl Hat Cuff
(13 x 4 threads)

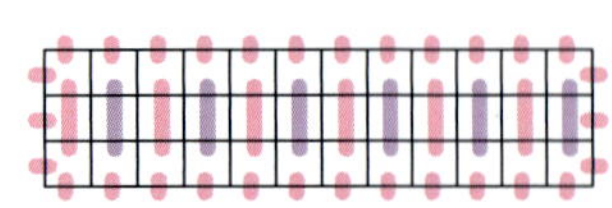

Snowlady Eye
(4 x 4 threads)
(stitch 2)

Snowlady Nose
(7 x 4 threads)

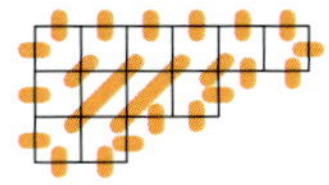

Snowlady Front/Back
(30 x 78 threads) (cut 2) (stitch 1)

Snowgirl Nose
(5 x 3 threads)

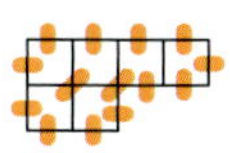

Earmuffs
(8 x 52 threads)

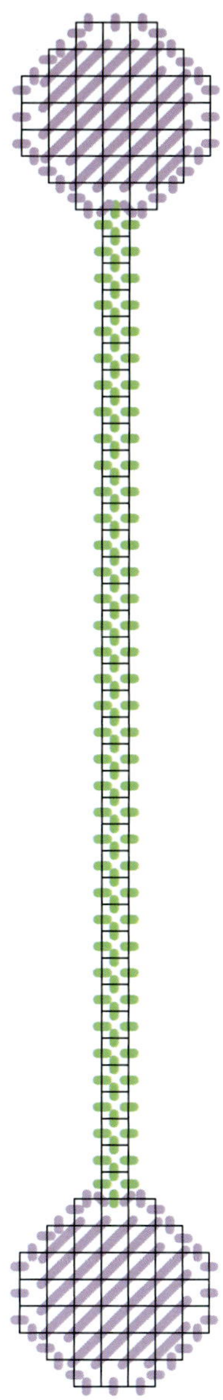

Snowgirl
(12 x 39 threads)

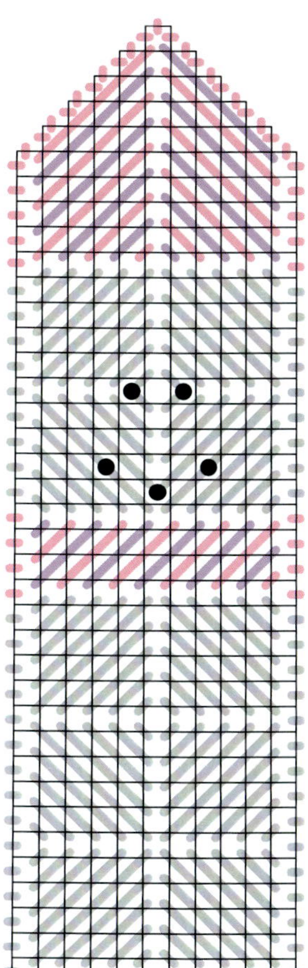

Continued on pg. 32.

KEY

COLOR
white
yellow
orange
pink
red
lt green
green
black
black Fr. knot

Star (10 x 10 threads)

Top Hat Snowman Eye
(4 x 4 threads) (stitch 2)

Top Hat Snowman Nose
(7 x 4 threads)

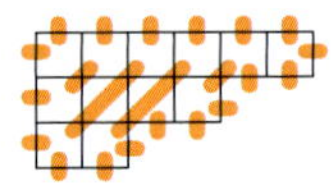

Red Bird Beak
(4 x 4 threads)

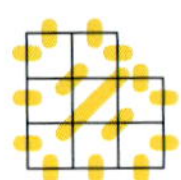

Red Bird Wing
(11 x 6 threads)

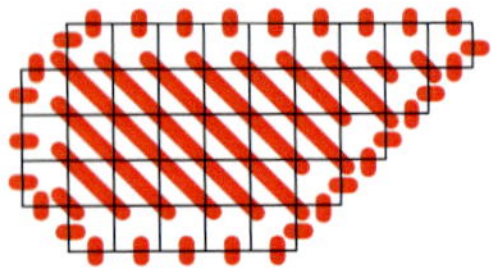

Red Bird
(17 x 17 threads)

Top Hat Snowman Front/Back
(30 x 90 threads) (cut 2) (stitch 1)

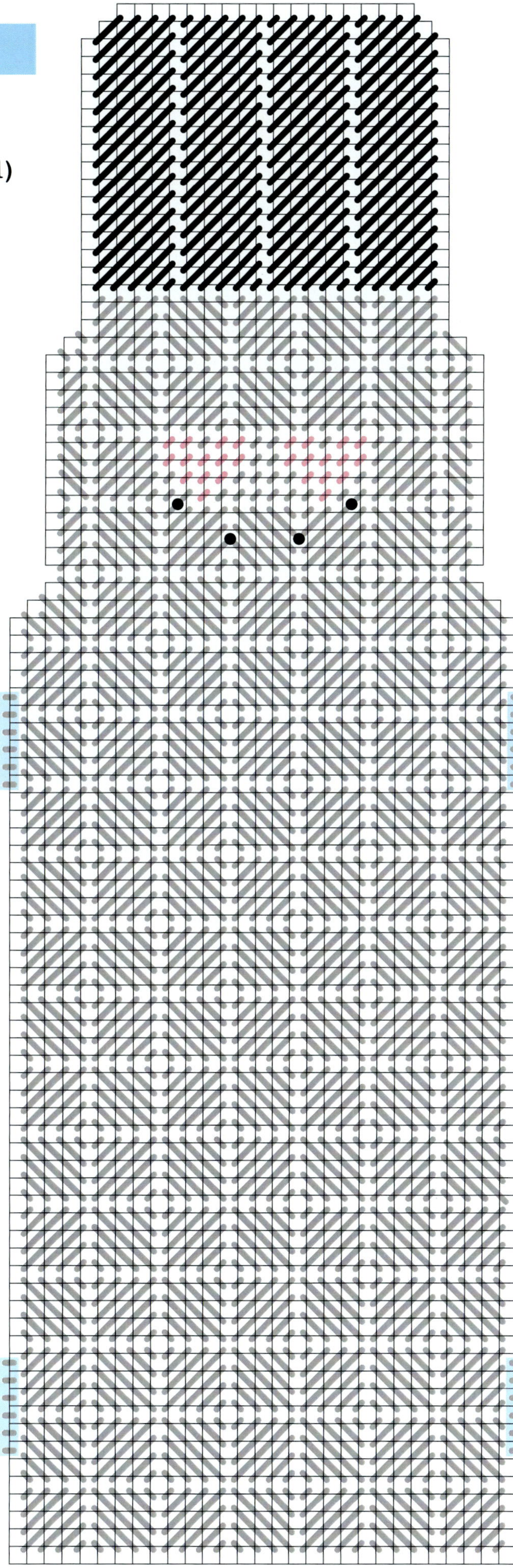

Top Hat Snowman Hat Brim
(32 x 7 threads)

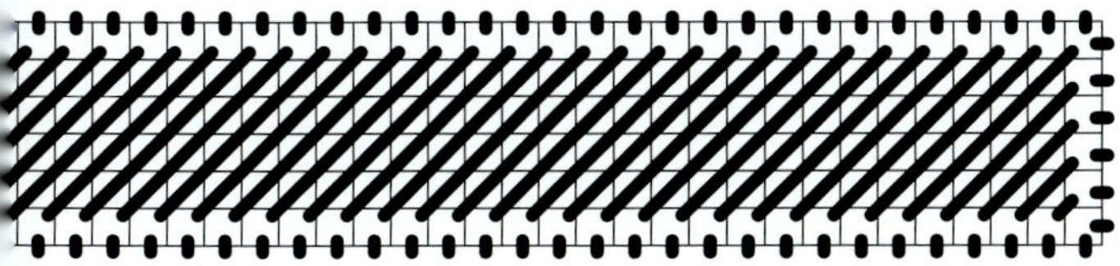

Top Hat Snowman Bow
(17 x 10 threads)

Top Hat Snowman Scarf
(30 x 9 threads)

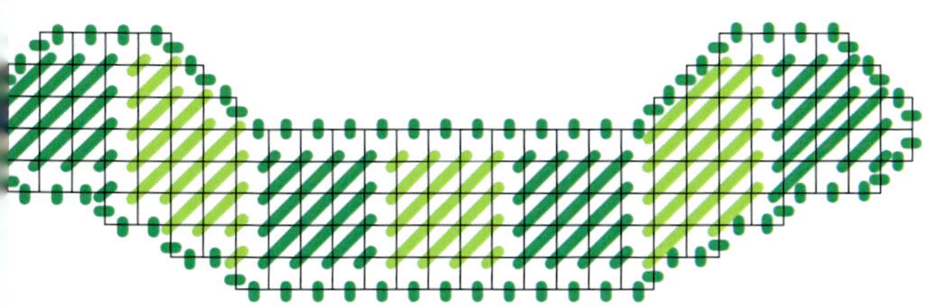

Continued on pg. 34.

Vested Snowman Eye
(4 x 4 threads) (stitch 2)

Vested Snowman Nose
(7 x 4 threads)

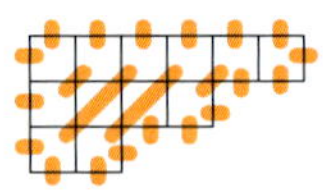

KEY

COLOR
white
yellow
orange
pink
red
lt blue
variegated blue
navy
brown
black
black Fr. knot

Small Heart
(6 x 5 threads)

Little Beak
(3 x 3 threads)

Little Blue Bird
(9 x 9 threads)

Little Wing
(6 x 4 threads)

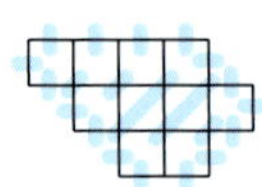

Birdhouse
(20 x 24 threads)

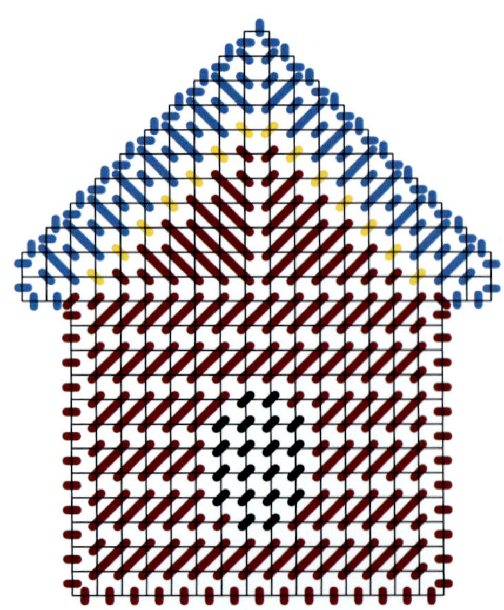

Vested Snowman Front/Back
(30 x 82 threads) (cut 2) (stitch 1)

Vested Snowman Hat Brim
(29 x 8 threads)

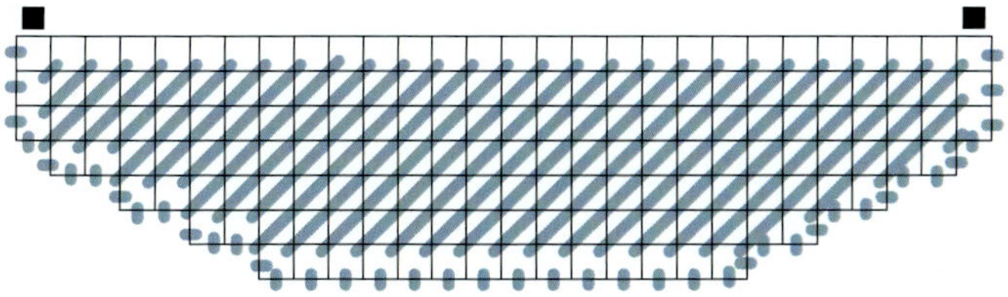

Vested Snowman Hat
(26 x 15 threads)

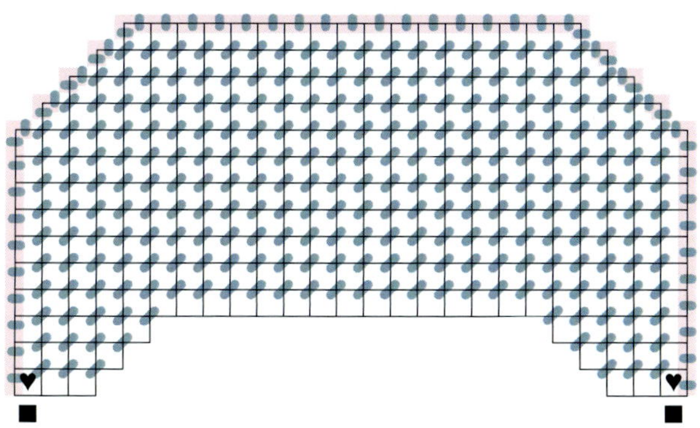

Vest Left Side
(14 x 19 threads)

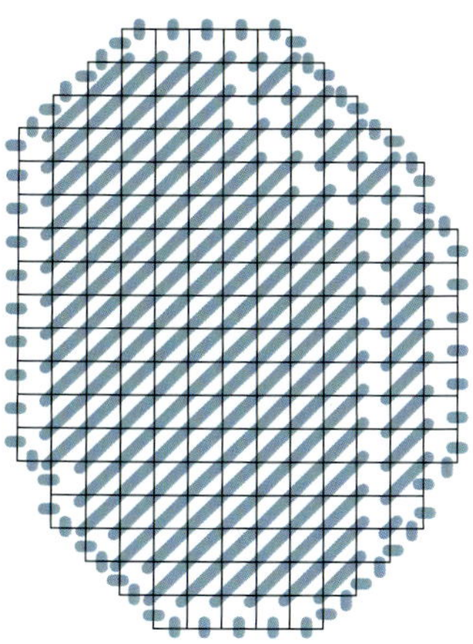

Vest Right Side
(14 x 19 threads)

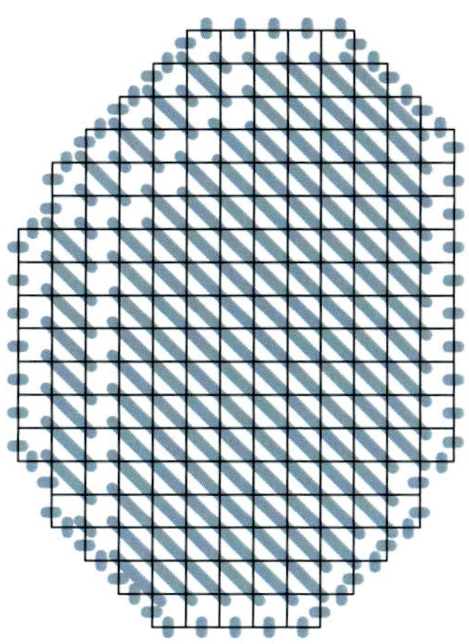

Show us what you're working on!

Share your project photos with us on social media.
Tag us @leisureartsinc or use #leisurearts

Production Team: Writer - Merrilee Gasaway; **Artist** – Wendy Willets; and **Photo Stylist** - Janna Laughlin.

Instructions tested and some cover items made by Carlene Hodge.

Made in U.S.A.